Endorsements

Regarding her first book, *Tidbits and Pearls: A Book of Essays on Living Everyday Life with God*:

Engaging stories, a wealth of insight, and a warm, assuring friend await you inside the pages of *Tidbits and Pearls*. Let Ladonna Shanks help you on your own journey as she shares so honestly from hers about following Jesus through the challenges and mundane realties of daily living. You'll find Jesus unveiling his wisdom for you too!

~ **Wayne Jacobsen**, author of HE LOVES ME, FINDING CHURCH, and A LANGUAGE OF HEALING FOR A POLARIZED NATION, and coauthor of THE SHACK

Sermons from a Soapbox

Sermons from a Soapbox is an inspiring collection of spiritual wisdom written with the finesse of one who has lived her eight decades with a completely teachable heart. Ladonna Shanks skillfully weaves what she has learned in her obedient soul, together with everyday experiences, in a way that every reader will appreciate. She illustrates how God is above, below, and in the midst of each one of life's events. In language everyone will find flowing, appealing, and instructional, she deftly draws us into a sphere of understanding that is rarely depicted by authors today. I highly recommend *Sermons from a Soapbox*.

~ **Gayle Carlson**, published Christian poet and member with Ladonna of Eugene, Oregon's Writers' Group PenPals

In Ladonna Shanks's second book, *Sermons from a Soapbox*, readers are enticed with her casual and wisdom-filled style. Her transparency encourages readers to have their own personal ah-ha moments while they read. The tone invites one to sit with a friend and reminisce over old times.

Sermons from a Soapbox is divided into three sections, each of which have pertinent essays. Unlike many memoirs, chapters are broken into short snippets of life, not necessarily in chronological order. One could open it at random and savor time with the author.

The book highlights applications from personal stories and leaves a legacy of lessons gleaned along life's journey. Skillfully woven snippets of life answer the question, "What is God trying to teach me in this situation?" Ladonna's transparency, while sharing fond, and not-so-fond, memories, invites the reader to walk beside her and reflect on life. After reading her book, you will want to meet the author!

~ **Robin Illers** has been writing poetry since she was in high school. Her first published poems appeared in her father's Foreign Language Department's newsletter, written in French under a pseudonym. She has also been published in *LIVE* and *The Standard*. She holds a master's degree in education, specializing in rehabilitation teaching for the blind and visually impaired.

When I read the introduction to Ladonna's book, I found myself smiling. Her grandfather's nickname for her described her youthful enthusiasm to live out her faith and to share the gospel with others. She has learned so many valuable lessons in her decades of living for Him, and she has learned the power of *being* rather than doing, trusting Him to reach hearts and transform lives. As I read this book, I found myself imagining having tea with her and enjoying meaningful conversations about so many aspects of the Christian life.

We live in a world where we are inundated with shallow conversations and opinions. But most of us long for an older friend, a mentor with whom we can discuss life. With the wisdom acquired from life, and the grace and kindness developed from walking with Jesus for many decades, Ladonna Shanks shares her thoughts about life's inevitabilities. In an age where absolute truth has been eroded, her voice matters. She takes us back to the carpenter's shop where Jesus built things along with His father, and she shares who He really is. Clearly, she knows and loves Jesus. In gentle and winsome ways, Ladonna has written a book that will encourage others to seek wisdom and most of all to develop a relationship with Christ, the Savior she clearly treasures. This book will be a blessing to many.

~ **Susan Kuenzi**, MS, retired counselor, writer, and founder of Tenderly Transformed Coaching, and follower of Christ.

Our heavenly Father is the creator of the universe and everything in our world. Sometimes this makes it hard to see Him in our daily walk. In *Sermons from a Soapbox*, Ladonna Shanks portrays not only the majesty of God but the everyday God who cares about each and every one of us. Reading this book definitely will encourage the reader to look for God our Father in daily living.

~ **Betty Hodges**, mother, grandmother, and great-grandmother. Betty earned an associate's degree from Linn-Benton Community College and wrote for the school's newspaper. During those college years and into retirement, she worked as a missionary alongside her husband pioneering the Adult and Teen Challenge PacNorthwest centers.

Imagine sitting on a porch swing each evening and listening to a friend share her deepest thoughts, convictions, and discoveries about God. "Wait," you might say. "How did you come to believe that?" As if in answer to your unexpressed questions, author Ladonna Shanks knits them together with stories from her life as a gardener, mother, grandmother, neighbor, and friend. She shares with firm conviction her experience of living with God.

In her previous book, *Tidbits and Pearls,* author Shanks wrote about God's desire for friendship. *Sermons from a Soapbox* takes us to the next step. Who is God? What is God like? What is life with God about?

In search of answers to these questions, be ready to probe deeply. But since she describes them as "messages of hope and encouragement," don't be afraid. You will find yourself nodding and smiling as you recognize yourself in so many of the stories. This book feels like sitting on that porch swing, lemonade in hand, and soaking up the wisdom from a friend about the possibilities of thriving in a life lived with God.

~ **Dorothy Roberts Cline**, author of Fall to Flight: An Alaska Eaglet's Story of Survival

Sometimes the dearest gifts come from the most unlikely places. An online friend asked me to read a manuscript she was planning to submit to a publisher. I have worked as an editor in the past and was looking for a distraction, having recently experienced some major changes in my life. What I thought was going to be a merely academic endeavor, correcting punctuation and suggesting minor rewrites, became a labor of love and self-healing.

Very often it is the little things in life that lead to the best heart changes. Ladonna Shanks has a real talent for seeing truth and wisdom in the details of everyday life. In *Sermons from a Soapbox*, she retells her observations and the experience she has gleaned. Written in short vignettes that are very accessible, Ms. Shanks welcomes us into the conversation with an open heart and mind.

I loved the short chapter format that allowed me to pick up or put down the book as my day required!

By the end of the task, my online friend became a kindred spirit. I truly believe every reader will find themselves in this book. Be prepared to laugh, nod, and even shed a few tears. Enjoy!

~ **Cathi MacMillan**, Chandler, Arizona, holds bachelor's degree from the University of Southern Maine and a master's in Curriculum Development and Instructional Leadership from University of New York at Albany. She has additional curriculum development training with *National Geographic* and *Time Magazine* and worked in curriculum development. She has written for SPECIAL PARENT magazine, giving parents of disabled students suggestions on how to survive the system.

Have you ever been eating the most amazing, dark, rich chocolate—you know the kind that hits every note of flavor you are craving, and you think, *The ideal pairing would be the "perfect" cup of coffee to sip with this*? Well, I have, and even though I have experienced the chocolate on occasion and I have had some amazing cups of coffee, I have never experienced them at the same time. In Ladonna Shanks's book *Sermons from a Soapbox*, I encountered this perfect clash of flavors as she shares the simplicity and ordinariness of daily life and the richness of God's presence as He walks with her through this here and now, everyday, ordinary life. She also invites you on this God journey and encourages you that you too can live this "with God" life. This book is not just to be read, but savored, pondered, and enjoyed to the fullest. Bon appétit!

~ **Michelle McAninch**, Emmett, Idaho, lifelong friend of the author, wife of fifty years, mother of three sons, with a passion and drive for seeking truth, God, and His Kingdom.

SERMONS FROM A SOAPBOX

Messages of Hope and Encouragement

Ladonna Shanks

SERMONS FROM A SOAPBOX: MESSAGES OF HOPE AND ENCOURAGEMENT
First edition. Copyright © 2025 by Ladonna Shanks

The information contained in this book is the intellectual property of Ladonna Shanks and is governed by United States and International copyright laws. All rights reserved. No part of this publication, either text or image, may be used for any purpose other than personal use. Therefore, reproduction, modification, storage in a retrieval system, or retransmission, in any form or by any means, electronic, mechanical, or otherwise, for reasons other than personal use, except for brief quotations for reviews or articles and promotions, is strictly prohibited without prior written permission by the author.

NO AI TRAINING: Without in any way limiting Ladonna Shanks's exclusive rights under copyright, any use of this publication to "train" generative artificial intelligence (AI) technologies to generate text is expressly prohibited. The author reserves all rights to license use of this work for generative AI training and development of machine learning language models.

Hardback ISBN: 979-8-9925840-0-4
Softcover ISBN: 979-8-9925840-1-1
eBook ISBN: 979-8-9925840-2-8

Cover Designed by Donna Gielow McFarland
Artwork by Janie Oviatt

Unless otherwise noted, Scripture quotations are taken from the New Revised Standard Version, Updated Edition (NRSVUE). Copyright © 2021 National Council of Churches of Christ in the United States of America. Used by permission. All rights reserved worldwide.

Scripture quotations marked CEV are taken from the *Contemporary English Version* (CEV)

Copyright © 1995 by American Bible Society. Used by permission. All rights reserved.

Scripture quotations marked GNT are taken from the Good News Translation® (Today's English Version, Second Edition) © 1992 American Bible Society. Used by permission. All rights reserved.

Scripture quotations marked KJV are taken from the King James Version.

Scripture quotations marked NKJV are taken from the New King James Version®. Copyright © 1982 by Thomas Nelson. Used by permission. All rights reserved.

Scripture quotations marked NLT are taken from the *Holy Bible*, New Living Translation, copyright © 1996, 2004, 2015 by Tyndale House Foundation. Used by permission of Tyndale House Publishers, Inc., Carol Stream, Illinois 60188. Used by permission. All rights reserved.

Scripture quotations marked NLV are taken from the New Life Version (NLV). Copyright © 1969, 2003 by Barbour Publishing, Inc. Used by permission. All rights reserved.

Scripture quotations marked RSV are taken from the Revised Standard Version of the Bible, copyright © 1946, 1952, and 1971 the Division of Christian Education of the National Council of the Churches of Christ in the United States of America. Used by permission. All rights reserved.

Scripture quotations marked TPT are taken from The Passion Translation®. Copyright © 2017, 2018 by Passion & Fire Ministries, Inc. Used by permission. All rights reserved. ThePassionTranslation.com.

Unless otherwise noted, definitions are from *Wiktionary: The Free Dictionary*, https://en.wiktionary.org/wiki/Wiktionary#English.

Acknowledgements

*For Bonnie Hamilton, who provided
motivation and inspiration when I had none.*

*Thanks to Robin, Sara, Grace, Jan, and Gayle —
my fellow PenPals writers;
Mary, my reliable go-to editor; Janie, the artist extraordinaire;
Donna, whose magic created a book from pictures and words;
Mitzi, my fellow sojourner and life-long sister/friend;
Nora, the one who introduced me to God almost sixty years ago;
my family, who support and love me in every venture I undertake;
and to my Heavenly Father for entrusting me with this gift.
May His purposes be accomplished and may He be honored
and glorified.*

Contents

Introduction xvii

I: Intro to God 101 1

On Life 3
Absolutes and Precepts 5
On Living *with* God 10
Becoming as a Little Child 12
Pictures vs. Reality 15
Hiding in Plain Sight 18
On the Heart and Salvation 21
On Being Spiritually Alive 26
On Being Open to God . . . or Not 29
On Saying "Yes" or "No" 31
On Ingratitude and Good Manners 33
The Earth Is *Not* the Center of the Universe 37
On Being Homogenized 41
Not of this World 43

II: Life and the Living of It 47

The Faint of Heart 49
For Your Eyes Only 53
On Doing Dishes by Hand 57
Being Schooled by a Child 61
Flex and Flow 63

On Change 65

On Stamina 68

On Caring 72

On Living with a Threat 75

How to Walk on Water 79

Just Keep Me Going 84

On an Anniversary 86

On Gliders and Thumpers and Other Differences 90

On Time and the Giving of It 93

On Stubbornness and Regret 97

My Rocking Chair Barometer and Worry 100

On Giving Thanks in Everything................................104

On Happiness vs. Joy 107

On a God Joy 111

Finding Solace at My Piano 115

On Gathering Together with Charlie 120

On Being a Representative 123

The Voice That Came Out of Nowhere 126

Live Life Like a Golfer 128

III: Food for Thought 131

On Being Human 133

On a Pair of Walking Shoes 136

A Majority of One 139

On Thinking for Yourself 142

On Being Real 144

On Weeds in Your Garden 147
On Priorities 151
On Choices 153
On Contrast and Comparison 157
On Clarity 160
Deep Cleaning 163
On Seeing 166
On Unbelief 169
On Cloud Covers, Vision, and Faith 173
On Being Grounded 176
On Things 183
On Storing Junk 187
On Creatures of Habit 190
On Looking Back 194
On Prayer: Just Ask with Your Heart 196
On Contentment 199
On Injury, Healing, and Scars 202
On Grievances and Healing 206
On Forgiveness and Healing 209
On Being Prepared 210
I Wonder 214
On What If? 218
On the Endgame 221
Do You Know My Father? 224
About the Author 225

Introduction

Describing herself as "a bulldog running along at the feet of Jesus, barking at what He doesn't like," Carrie Amelia Nation, an American woman born in 1846, felt she was divinely ordained to promote temperance by destroying drinking establishments. Her methods for accomplishing this started with simple protests as she serenaded saloon patrons with hymns while playing a hand organ. Her efforts escalated when she began marching into bars, singing and praying while smashing bar fixtures and stock with a hatchet.

A woman passionate about her beliefs, she was arrested some thirty times between 1900 and 1910 for her "hatchetations," as she called them. While her anti-alcohol demonstrations did little to stem the tide of its use, abuse, and the resulting effect on society, her cause and name became part of our nation's history, originating in a time when the spread of information was limited to word of mouth, letters, and newspapers—no small thing since she is still remembered more than a century later.

I can relate to Carrie Nation's vigorous approach as she attempted to bring about change in the world she lived in. Early in my spiritual life, with conviction and in ardor, I felt it necessary to impose *my* beliefs upon others. Filled with a passion to save humanity from a fate of hell and damnation, I evangelized with boldness and force.

As a child, my grandfather didn't call me by my given name. He attached the moniker "Carrie Nation" to me. I wonder if the force of my personality and character manifested even as a small child. Grandpa's nickname, "Carrie Nation," suited me perfectly.

Entering high school, I could only be classed as "odd man out." My country grade school had an eighth grade graduating class of six. The high school enrollment of one thousand students catapulted me into culture shock. Many of my fellow classmates attended grade school and the same junior high together. I knew very few of them. If that wasn't enough to isolate me, my behavior, which could only be viewed as eccentric or fanatical, did.

A few months prior to that initiation into the larger world of high school campus life, I made a commitment to live my life for God. I thought He wanted and expected me to "be a witness." I walked alone from class to class, my Bible prominently displayed atop my books. While others socialized in the cafeteria and halls, I attended Bible Club during lunch hour. I doubt my actions affected change, though—not that much different from Carrie Nation with her hatchet.

As a young married woman, my concept of evangelism continued playing a major part in the way I lived as I strove to be the "perfect" Christian. I filled the role of church pianist, organized Vacation Bible School, and taught a Sunday school class. I led a youth group, attended Bible studies, and chaired an interdenominational women's group.

Then a friend introduced me to God, the person of God. Not doctrines, concepts, or ideas *about* Him, but Him—the one true living God. The direction of my life and how I lived it forever changed.

God desires a relationship with us, His creation. "All I have asked you to do is to live your life," He whispered. Over time, I learned He has not given me the role or responsibility to save the world. That belongs to Him. He only asked me to *be*. His plan, His way means visible, undeniable evidence of Him is revealed as I live life. It *is* a better way.

In creating *Sermons from a Soapbox*, I compiled essays I have written over several years. They are not presented in any particular chronological order, so you can peruse the contents and select a message that piques your curiosity or perhaps fits a current situation. These are not sermons where I tell you, the reader, what to do or how to live, but, rather, a sharing: of myself and my thoughts; of life with God; of His goodness, kindness, and mercy; of Him. I feel it is a superior alternative to the Carrie Nation approach. May your mind and heart be pointed to God as you allow me to "preach" from my soapbox.

If you have not considered it before, I encourage you to contemplate living in the eternal, spiritual reality, not just in this physical, material world.

And may your spirit resonate with the truth of God's love for humankind and His desire to be our friend.

Author's note: The sketch used for the cover was created from a photo of myself standing in front of my dad's barn. The red rose was added in memory of my mother and her favorite rose, "Mom's Rose." ~ Ladonna Shanks

I
Intro to God 101

*"I am the Alpha and Omega," says the Lord God,
who is and who was and who is to come, the Almighty.*
Revelation 1:8

On Life

life: n. The state of being alive and living. A living individual; the fact of a particular individual being alive.

Life. We have all been given the gift of life.

I struggle finding the words to express the individuality and uniqueness of every person created by God. Humankind can honestly be compared to the one-of-a-kind snowflakes that fall, singular yet never duplicated. Ever. What a mind-blowing, profound concept! I become confounded when I try to wrap my mind around the originality of each of us. Every person matters, created with value and purpose from a mind and heart of love. No duplicates exist—only one "you" has been created. And only one "me."

For years I wrestled with that age-old question, "What is the meaning of life?" In essence, I questioned my existence and purpose. God made the difference for me when He quietly spoke, "That you might know Me, the one and only true living God."

As I share my thoughts and life with you, I may come across as one standing on a soapbox. That is not my intention. I weigh my words carefully. I don't want you to feel I preach at you.

My desire is that each of you might come to know God as you experience life and a relationship with Him. That kind of life brings meaning and purpose.

Allow your mind and heart to open up as you read. And may these words and God's spirit continue to point you to a life in sync with Him, one worth living, as He reveals Himself to you, and you come to know Him more fully.

Absolutes and Precepts
The Basics of God

absolute: n. That which is independent of context-dependent interpretation, inviolate, fundamental. adj. Certain, not to be doubted.

precept: n. A rule for action or behavior, esp. one based on moral consideration.

Absolutes make up the foundation of our planet, its functions, and cycles:

Each and every day, with surety, the ocean's tide rises and falls.

Without exception, in a journey of approximately 365 days planet Earth rotates on its axis while circling the sun, the center of our solar system.

Weather remains a daily constant in the lives of humankind. While often unpredictable, and despite its importance in our lives, we hold no authority over it. Instead, every facet of weather regularly controls and influences us — how and where we live, our activities, the clothing we wear, and our emotional and physical well-being too.

Every day, physical life begins when an egg and sperm meet, conception takes place, and a new life is created. The mother's womb provides a cocoon for development and growth. Months later, when enough time has passed and life can survive independently, birth takes place.

On the other end of the spectrum, physical life ends daily worldwide. Death may be due to age, tragedy, or a malady, but its inevitability for all who live cannot be avoided.

These are absolutes. They are also realities of life.

When scientists launch a space shuttle, construct an underwater tunnel, investigate wildlife in a jungle, or plan and initiate a plethora of projects *ad infinitum*, these and multitudinous other absolutes must be acknowledged.

Science serves as both an observer and a discoverer. Whether considering the natural sciences (biology, chemistry, and physics), or the formal sciences (logic, mathematics, and computer science), the whole of science falls under the governance and control of all the absolutes of creation and must operate within those bounds and limitations.

The scientific world often presents itself as opposing and challenging God, placing the burden of proof upon Him to prove His very existence. However, even if that world and those in it do not believe in God as Creator, they still function because of Him. Science may reject the Creator, but it cannot ignore the absolute exactness and precision of all His creation. Absolutes govern the operation of our world and will not be spurned.

Just as facts of science must be reckoned with, the same applies to truths about God, His personality, and His nature. These precepts pertaining to Him are particularly pertinent. And they are absolute . . . as He is absolute. In the same way He will never change, these principles will never change.

God is love. All that He does comes from that base.

#1: *All* things are spiritual; things are not as they seem to be.

God, the Creator, stands as the cornerstone of everything in this life, world, galaxy, and universe. Because He is, by nature, a spiritual being, all things come from a spiritual base, not a physical one. Since we live in His world, we need to have spiritual vision in order to have a clear view of life.

Observing life any other way resembles looking at a black-and-white photograph of a sunset. One can clearly see the basic form but none of the color or the beauty. You can look at it yet not really see it. God's wisdom, foresight, intelligence, and thought go into the base construct and fabric of the mundane experiences in our everyday lives. Multi-faceted and dimensional, He creates them for discipline, a lesson, or a crossroads — all part of the whole of life, designed by the One who made us. Because He is spiritual, they are spiritual.

#2: First things first. The inner must be dealt with first. Then the outer. The outer without the inner is worthless.

A person's spiritual being, the inner, dwells deep within, unseen and invisible to human eyes. Our physical body makes up the outer. While humankind can alter or manipulate the outer body, God alone can develop the spiritual part of us, our inner self, which is by far the most important. When we focus only on the outer, we create a very fragile shell that will collapse under the slightest bit of pressure.

#3: If you don't make a decision, the decision is made for you.

People often want to postpone the consideration of God in their lives to "someday." Fear often suggests that God will interfere, playing into the minds of those driven and motivated by the desire to live life "my way." Therefore, many undertake a genuine effort to keep Him at bay. "Yes" or "No." In or out. "Someday" cannot be considered an option. Opportunities don't last forever. If you ignore them, you will be left out.

#4: If you wait to see, you've waited too long.

"I'll believe it when I see it." This position carries serious ramifications since one never knows when life will come to an end. If you live with this philosophy, a hefty price will be exacted. No possibility exists to repeat life.

#5: There is a better way.

Two ways exist in life — our way and God's way. His way *is* better. It doesn't get any simpler than that.

#6: There are no skipped steps. There are no shortcuts.

Life will be lived. Lessons will be taught in the order planned and designed by the Master. He does not play leapfrog.

#7: Just keep going.

Curling up in a fetal position or sitting down in protest accomplishes nothing and serves no purpose. Regardless of how difficult circumstances may be, that which God begins He also completes. Moving forward, then, has to be the best approach — one step at a time.

#8: He's not a moment too soon, not a moment too late.

Timing. It's always about the timing. No one has better timing than God. His is perfect.

#9: Stay in your own yard.

Mind your own business. Each of us has more than enough on our own plate so that it behooves us to focus on those things that only involve us personally. Stepping outside that space generally comes from a place of judgment, ego, or the desire or effort to do God's work for Him. It is never productive.

#10: Do not add to; do not take away from.

God means what He says and says what He means. When you have difficulty understanding, ask what He means. Applying self-reasoning to anything He says sits right up there as the equivalent of running on a hamster wheel going nowhere fast.

#11: In order to become a teacher, one must be willing to be taught.

No substitute replaces the time spent as a student. I cannot teach what I have not learned. And under the tutelage of God, the learning never ends.

Absolutes. Precepts. Words to live by.

Feast on them. Absorb them. Consider them before God.

On Living *with* God

How *does* a person live with God? We know Him to be omnipotent, omniscient, the great I AM. God is love. He ascribes the name Alpha and Omega to Himself, the beginning and the end. As mere mortals, we pale in comparison to His immortality.

God desires friendship and a relationship with us, His creation. Any friendship entails a process, that of getting acquainted with and learning about one another, long before coming to a point of total and complete trust. Shared experiences reveal facets that affect the likelihood of that friendship moving forward or disintegrating. Trust must be earned. That same process applies to God.

Bear in mind we have been created in the image of God. We possess emotions, personality, a sense of humor, attributes, traits, and characteristics that are individually and uniquely ours. Because *He* does.

The single-word descriptions of God are valid but also one-dimensional. They do not begin to present the multiple facets of Him. I desire to share small nuggets of the person of God with you. Reason requires that I note I have limited experience. I'm not suggesting I know Him in His fullness. I do not. No person can. But I do know Him better than when I began my journey with Him more than seventy-five years ago.

What is God like?

God is God. What a paradox that He chose us to be His friends! We are unworthy, yet of such worth He provided a way for us to have life, not only in our present state but for all eternity. We are all that is unholy, yet His work within us cleanses. We are unrighteous, yet He has provided righteousness for us so we can live with Him.

God does not change to live with humankind. *We* must change to live with Him. That change can only happen at His hand as He disciplines, molds, and shapes each of us into the person He created us to be, so we might live in freedom with Him.

As you enter into a friendship with God, the Lord of all the universe, be prepared for discovery. Your mind will be blown wide open as you find, on many levels, He challenges your perceptions and ideas about Him, regardless of an earlier church experience or lack thereof.

Join me as I share some personal experiences and insights into living daily life with God. May you see He does not want "perfect" people. He does desire contrite, open, honest folk who want to live a better life, one in sync with Him — those who come to Him as a little child.

I pray He ends up being your best friend.

Becoming as a Little Child

He felt exhausted, bone-weary. The clamor and crush of the crowds drained His body, mind, and spirit. He did not question His calling and purpose. Yet there were times when Jesus longed for the solace of the shop.

The carpentry shop had occupied His being as an important part of His life since childhood. The memory of the smell of wood chips carpeting the floor filled His soul. The young Jesus had a favorite spot where He perched, out of the way, so He could watch his earthly father, Joseph, deal with the rough logs he had sawn. Before long, His father began mentoring Him in the skills of the trade.

In adulthood, as a trained tradesman, He converted chunks of wood into creations of utility and beauty with His hands, before His eyes, just as Joseph did. His Heavenly Father taught Him there too, preparing Him for what lay ahead. The shop served as His refuge, a place of peace.

His physical body exuded strength with taut, sinewy muscles developed by wielding the primitive hand tools of His time. He had a fit spiritual body too, one strong enough to face and withstand evil in its rawest form.

The life of the carpenter's son, Jesus of Nazareth, had changed dramatically. He knew when it happened. His baptism by John the Baptist, His cousin, marked the turning point. The heavens opened, and the Holy Spirit descended upon Him like a dove. An audible pronouncement followed: "You are My beloved Son, in whom I am well pleased."[1]

Jesus's daily life included miracles and signs as His three-year ministry on earth began. Masses of people followed Him wherever He went. They craved His teaching, brought those who were sick to be healed, and sought deliverance from demons. He knew He was sent for humankind. Nevertheless, the daily rigor and relentless demands became tiring, with places and times of retreat minimal.

The children delighted Him. They brought a smile to His face. Their purity and honesty made Him laugh. He loved watching them and enjoyed hearing their conversations as they played. They didn't test Him with religious or political questions. They didn't ask Him to prove anything, demanding to know who He was or why He had come. They didn't bait Him with verbal traps.

Parents brought their little ones to Him, asking for His blessing. The disciples who followed along beside Him wanted to send them away, but Jesus chastised them: "Let the little children come to Me and do not forbid them."[2]

When His disciples expressed concern about *their* personal status in the kingdom of heaven (each of them seeking a superior position), Jesus called a small child to come sit in the middle of them. He delivered His assessment: "Truly I tell you, unless you change and become like children, you will never enter the kingdom of heaven. Whoever becomes humble like this child is the greatest in the kingdom of heaven."[3]

---

[1] Mark 1:11 NKJV
[2] Matthew 19:14 NKJV
[3] Matthew 18:3–4

Becoming as a little child. What, exactly, does that mean?

Children live in the moment. They do not know political correctness and express their emotions freely. Even the youngest instinctively gauge those they allow into their world. In succinct terms, they trust with their heart and do not rely on their mind.

Many of life's struggles take place in the mind. Children have yet to be encumbered by the mental process of thought. They simply trust. How hard can that be? Very hard for some, easy for others.

Note the following perspective of a child: "I don't understand why all people don't just follow God. It's so easy." What wisdom. At the ripe old age of eight, she is a living example of the very thing I am trying to express.

While children have no understanding of the meaning of the word *trust*, they ultimately represent it as they live under the care of a loving parent, without fear, doubt, or questioning. Some may view this as naïve, lacking intellectual maturity, but we should model them in their direct, simple approach to life.

No decision carries more gravity and importance than choosing to humble oneself and place trust in God instead of self. The choice belongs to each of us, and the results of that choice have long-term ramifications.

Consider the need to become as a little child.

"For it is to such as these that the kingdom of heaven belongs."
Matthew 19:14

Pictures vs. Reality

picture: n. An image; a representation in the imagination.

reality: n. The state of being actual or real.

Recently, an acquaintance called me "a hippy girl." While I hold no personal bias against hippies, and the term *was* intended as a compliment, the description collided head-on with a picture I've carried in my mind for years.

In my imagination, I hold an image of becoming a lady, a *sophisticate* even—someday, mind you. The fantasy of fulfillment sits in place right alongside the picture.

I can hear family members and those who know me and my lifestyle roar with laughter, as I am anything and everything but . . . a lady, that is.

A persistent problem exists with pictures. They lack anything real. Manufactured in one's imagination, they tend to hang around in the mind for a long period of time. We replay them over and over like an old, favorite movie, frequently editing as we color, shade, and alter them. After creating an image that suits us, usually one that feels quite warm and fuzzy, we end up with our own fabricated, "pretty" picture.

Each of us possesses a secret, personal photo album rolling around within the inner recesses of our mind. No one sees it or even knows of its existence unless we decide to share with them.

How many of us had a picture of parenthood *before* children? Maybe of retirement or a new job? Perhaps of a vacation trip, a holiday with the family, a new pet, a change in lifestyle, a relationship. Need I go on? When reality enters and takes over, the comments usually begin with "I thought" and end with "but . . ."

Tomorrow holds only unknowns, and we may deal with it by filling in the blanks, imagining our future and how it might play out.

Drum roll, please. Enter reality. Sooner or later our pictures will always collide with reality. Without fail, reality will prevail.

I maintain humankind possesses pictures of God as well, and those pictures have nothing to do with reality. We have ideas and perceptions about Him and what He will or won't do. We believe them and state them as absolutes. How do I know? Charge me with being the worst offender.

I challenge you to find the truth about Him for yourself. You might be pleasantly surprised. I was. He doesn't abide by any of the rules I *thought* He did. He does not play games or manipulate. He's not "out to get us." He desires friendship, giving us the opportunity to become part of His world and His eternal Kingdom.

You can be as straightforward and direct as asking Him, "What are You really like?" I began my quest with that question.

What do you have to lose? A lot of pictures. What do you have to gain? Truth and reality.

Back to the evaporation of my picture, the *sophisticate*. In truth, I talk far too loudly, laugh with too much fervor, and walk with too much force to ever be considered a lady. I have zero poise, and I dress and work like the gardener I am. The imagined "lady" has never been in my DNA, and, as I enter my elder years, even my prettiest picture will never come to pass.

At this point in life, I feel I need to embrace the reality of that hippy girl. Besides, a lady wouldn't be caught dead wearing the big, floppy gardening hat I love.

Hiding in Plain Sight

geocaching: n. A pastime in which participants use a GPS receiver to find a hidden container at a specific latitude and longitude or to hide a container to be found in this manner.

The grocery store parking lot bustled with shoppers and cars during the busiest time of the day as I wandered around, digging through the shrubbery. The heat, the sight of the syringe, and the futility of my efforts dampened my enthusiasm for geocaching, at least for the moment.

I knew I had narrowed down the hiding place for the cache since the clue *Caching in the Lamplight* and information on my phone indicated I was within two feet of the treasure. After I circled the lamp post in the middle of the lot for the hundredth time—well, not quite, but enough to feel quite foolish and hope no one noticed, I concluded someone had come along and stolen the find. That was my story, and I stuck to it.

My adult children and grandchildren introduced me to geocaching. The activity can be described as a treasure hunt of sorts, where the goal and accomplishment culminate in finding a hidden cache. The new smart phones simplify the search, making it user-friendly for folk of all ages, young and old alike. People have hidden more than two million caches worldwide, most of them small trinkets. When you find one, you sign the physical logbook in the cache container, replace the treasure with one of your own, and return the container to its hiding place. You may then record your success online. I had never attempted a geocache alone before. I knew the cache had to be hiding in plain sight. I just couldn't find it.

My son discovered it within thirty seconds when he lifted the metal collar on the post. He sent me a picture to verify the feat. Armed with some visible assistance, I headed back and found it myself. It was, indeed, hiding in plain sight.

When the space exploration program got underway several decades ago, astronauts were given the charge to look for God while on their outer space mission. Simple, silly humans with their minds all askew. No one will find God "out there." He can be found right here. Everywhere. "As plain as the nose on your face," my mom would say. As with the cache, one just needs to know where to look.

How do you find someone hiding in plain sight, especially God? I believe the answer to that question goes back to a person's heart. If one sincerely desires to see God, to find and to know Him, they will. The key: purity of heart. "Blessed are the pure in heart, for they will see God."[4]

I will probably try to find another cache, armed and emboldened with one semi-successful solo geocaching experience. However, geocaching will never compare to the search for, and resulting find of, the One hiding in plain sight. One falls in the category of "fun and recreational." The other is invaluable, life-enriching, and eternal—a priceless treasure.

---

[4] Matthew 5:8

*"Ask, and it will be given to you;
search, and you will find;
knock, and the door will be opened for you."*
Matthew 7:7

On the Heart and Salvation

salvation: n. The process of being saved, the state of having been saved (from hell).

Have you ever heard of a midden? Do you know its purpose? Do you understand and can you explain crop rotation or stock futures? How about symbiotic relationships or drying out? These terms may be unfamiliar since they relate to specific lines of work, endeavors, or interests, each with their own unique, specific vocabulary. If you don't know the meaning of the words, you might as well be listening to a foreign language.

Schooling in any field, whether physical in nature or intellectual, includes teaching the language, its definitions, and practical applications. For example, an electrician will talk about circuits and amperes, insulators and hertz, whereas an archaeologist may speak of artifacts, grids, or a midden, a space set aside for trash disposal. Medical terminology is the jargon the medical world uses to describe the body, its functions, and the treatments they prescribe. Every area of life has its own definitive vocabulary, whether in sports, banking, real estate, politics, parenting, or education.

Religion and all spiritual things do not differ. Salvation, the heart of man, eternal life — what do these terms mean?

I grew up in a conservative home and attended an evangelical church with my parents. I have no memory of life before church. A basic foundational doctrine of my childhood religious education emphasized my need for salvation. In accordance with the teaching of the church, "inviting Jesus into my heart" fulfilled that necessity. As a youngster, I often reflected on how that could be possible. Mentally, I peered into my inner self, trying to locate my heart and ascertain: How could Jesus dwell there?

Much of religious life takes place in the head. Those in authority often present doctrines as the gospel truth, with no room for questioning or challenges. Religious peers and superiors may expect obedience as proof of faithfulness. Sometimes, you will find the path to Christianity laid out in a few easy steps, followed by a collection plate. The list of accepted and required behavior can be quite long, often with more "don'ts" than "dos."

Spiritual life and religious life are not one and the same. Spiritual life, based on a relationship with God, emanates from one's spiritual heart. The other takes place in the outer — satisfying doctrines, rules, and requirements.

The complexity of human creation cannot be overstated: Body. Soul. Heart. Mind. Daily, as we live our lives, we experience the specialized role of each of these facets as well as their ability to coordinate, one with another.

Our physical house contains our flesh-and-blood body. Our soul harbors our personality and makeup, which consists of unique, individual traits. It *is* the essence of who we are. My soul is *me*. Thoughts and reasoning take place in the mind. We process ideas there, make judgments and assessments, and come to conclusions. In our minds, we make decisions in concert with our soul.

We have been created with both a physical and a spiritual heart. The physical heart, a muscular organ, pumps blood through the body, sending it to the brain and other vital organs. Many folks tend it through exercise and health in an effort to extend physical life. Medical specialists can even replace a faulty heart by means of a heart transplant. When the physical heart stops beating, life as we know it comes to an end.

Where does one find the spiritual heart? And what, exactly, is it? A person's spiritual heart will never show up on an X-ray or MRI. No instrument can check its health, pressure, or rate of beating. And yet we all have one. The way we live our lives indicates whether our hearts have been touched by God's hand. Or not.

God created humans with the knowledge of His existence. The spiritual heart harbors the seat of an awareness and consciousness of God, our Creator. "In reality, the truth of God is known instinctively, for God has embedded this knowledge inside every human heart."[5]

When Adam and Eve disobeyed God in the Garden of Eden and ate of the fruit of the tree of the knowledge of good and evil, the heart was cursed, left in need of redemption. "For from within, out of the heart of men, proceed evil thoughts, adulteries, fornications, murders, thefts, covetousness, wickedness, deceit, lewdness, an evil eye,

---

[5] Romans 1:19 TPT

blasphemy, pride, foolishness. All these evil things come from within and defile a man."[6]

As we acknowledge God and the provisional sacrifice of His Son, a cleansing takes place in the spiritual heart, changing it from its state of depravity and making it new. Only He can do this work. If that does not take place, the condition of rot and decay remain. "Create in me a clean heart, O God, and put a new and right spirit within me."[7]

I have discovered the location of my heart, my spiritual heart. It dwells in the very core of my being, deep within me, invisible to the naked eye. No foe, human or spiritual, can touch or damage it.

My spiritual heart is alive, because the Spirit of God quickened it and made it His home. He fills me with His presence and His knowledge there. He teaches me and gives me understanding.

In the same way my physical heart pumps life-giving blood through my body, God's Spirit pumps life into and through my spiritual heart. A renewed spiritual heart is the ultimate heart transplant. And, unlike a physical heart, it will continue on into eternity.

And that, my friend, is salvation. That simple. That complex. That true.

May each of you have the eternal, life-giving experience of a renewed heart. Seek God with your body, soul, heart, and mind.

---

[6] Mark 7:21–23 NKJV
[7] Psalm 51:10

*For it is by believing in your heart
that you are made right with God,
and it is by openly declaring your faith
that you are saved.*
Romans 10:10 NLT

On Being Spiritually Alive

spiritual: adj. Of or pertaining to the spirit or the soul; not material.

physical: adj. Having to do with the body, the material world.

The look on her face personified petrified fear, a frozen expression of sheer terror. It could accurately be compared to that of the proverbial deer with its eyes "caught in the headlights." I have no doubt my own face mirrored hers as I slammed on my brakes. The older woman riding a bicycle lost her balance as she stopped on the sidewalk and dismounted—directly in front of my truck. Giving me one of those "if looks could kill" glares, she got back on and rode off, seething with anger. I saw her mouth an expletive. I couldn't say I blamed her.

Accessing the street via an alley, a large climbing rose blocked my vision. Fortunately for both of us, I was at a virtual crawl as I moved forward. The woman hadn't seen me, and I didn't see her, until we were face-to-face. Even at my very slow speed, I was a split-second away from knocking her down. She didn't have a helmet on. The situation could have easily become calamitous.

I pulled out onto the street, drove down a block, and turned onto a side street, waiting for her to ride by. Rolling down my window, I shouted, "I am sooo sorry." Her anger evaporated as the two of us agreed with a thumbs-up, "It's all good."

As I headed to my next gardening job, my being once again filled with gratitude to God for His presence in my day-to-day existence.

There is *physical*. And then there is *spiritual*.

We all know what it means to have a physical life. What does it mean to have a spiritual life? How does that differ? *Does* it make a difference? And does it matter?

Certain types of practices, such as wearing specific types of clothing, stopping to pray five times a day, completing classes of doctrine, or living a monastic life of celibacy and fasting, setting aside certain days as sacred, adhering to a dietary standard, or following rules define religion. One can be very religious and yet spiritually dead.

How does one who is spiritually dead become spiritually alive?

We humans possess no more capability of creating life in the spiritual realm than we can in the physical world. Becoming spiritually alive, a spiritual birth, takes place when a person opens up their innermost self to God and invites Him in. He quickens our spirit, giving it life, and, in that process, He becomes part of us.

He is light, life, and truth. You will also find Him to be a true gentleman. He never goes anywhere uninvited.

Everyday life with God is far removed from being idyllic—filled with fairy tales of the hereafter, balloons, and lullabies. For me, that perception fell apart with the statement, "God does not keep you from hard times. He *does* walk with you as you go through them." His support and companion-ship in difficult circumstances establishes just one reason being spiritually alive matters.

Another reason: He choreographs every step of life, including a near-disastrous encounter with a woman on a bike. God, my Creator, knows me, loves me, and has my best interest at heart. Living alone on my own doesn't hold a candle to that arrangement.

All things physical are temporary. All things spiritual are eternal. And that makes being spiritually alive the most important reason of all.

If there is a physical body, there is also a spiritual body.
1 Corinthians 15:44

On Being Open to God . . . or Not

"You know," my friend announced assertively, "it's all about being open." Standing in her kitchen, preparing dinner, she continued. "If you want to live your life with God, you just have to be open to Him." (This young woman has always been one to tell it like it is.)

Five main religions dominate in the United States. Using the definition of religion as "any specific system of belief about deity; often involving rituals, a code of ethics, a philosophy of life, and a worldview," they include Christianity, Judaism, Islam, Buddhism, and Hinduism.

A 2020 poll reported that seven out of ten Americans identified as Christian. The Christianity sector includes at least thirty-five different denominations. In days gone by, religious training was often confined to a Sunday service along with a study group or training sessions midweek. That has changed with the advent of twenty-four-hours-a-day, seven-days-a-week television and the internet, where a plethora of religious programming can be found.

In a competition for viewers, which often translates into financial supporters, a deluge of words, along with a variety of doctrines, floods the land. Many of the preachers offer "how-to" prayers, explaining "how to" be saved and healed, or even "how to" find happiness and financial success. Of course, this is all done in the name of God. Man's version of God often overshadows any truth or reality as He gets buried in the clutter, bearing no resemblance to the purported image.

This contradicts God and His way. A massive sales campaign is the antithesis of God and not His style.

He asks that His people live their lives in a manner that draws others, not dissimilar to a moth being drawn to a flame. Those of faith need to be ready to answer if questioned about Him and about their beliefs.

For those who do not want God and want nothing to do with Him, I can categorically and emphatically state God will never impose Himself upon anyone. He does desire a relationship, but your free will rules. He will approach you in that quiet place within, but if you say "No," He *never* forces. He has true class and will not go anyplace where the welcome mat isn't out.

The *caveat*, however, is you must live with your decision. When the mountains begin to fall and when, at the end of this mortal life, you step into eternity and things aren't as you expected, planned, or hoped they would be, you will be left with your "free will" choice. No redo exists.

Stand. He asks that each of us simply stand by the decision we have made. Stand and live in it—and, eventually, die in it.

For those who want nothing to do with God, take comfort in the fact that He gives that freedom and that right. He will have nothing to do with you then. For those who do want Him, all you have to do is be open to Him, and He will share Himself with you as you live your life.

God is love, and He loves us enough to give us the freedom to choose.

On Saying "Yes" or "No"

The invitation included a request for acknowledgement of attendance—a simple "yes" or "no." I struggled making the decision. I would have to travel some distance to the event and, as a gardener, would also need to juggle and adjust my work schedule. The employee count in my business consists of me, myself, and I, so the postponed work would be waiting when I returned. In the end I knew I did not want to live with the regret of missing out, of being included yet refusing the invitation. As for the work, as my mother always said, "It'll keep."

I responded: "Yes, thank you."

How do choices, making decisions, and having the free will to do so apply to a relationship with an omnipotent and omniscient God? Understanding this can be difficult.

God's desire for friendship remains the basis of life with Him. His longing to have a friend culminated in the creation of man. The God of the universe, the one and only true living God, wants you, and He wants me, to be His friend. Given that, He will never force Himself upon anyone. He doesn't operate that way.

Consider a friendship, a relationship where mutual, genuine care and concern thrive. A friend will provide their input and opinion as you approach a situation. In making my decision, a close friend gave me her perspective. She never told me what to do but offered support and insight. My Heavenly Father did the same.

Knowing *about* another person does not create an open, honest relationship. *Knowing* them does. Religious groups often place focus and emphasis on learning *about* God and compiling information through Bible studies or sermons. At best, that can only be viewed as a tenuous prospect, as churches present Him in a variety of lights, depending upon their doctrine.

God's character, nature, and personality are revealed as He partners with me in life. I learn about myself too as honest interaction takes place.

He will, and He does, approach us, seeking friendship and the opportunity to get to know Him. Our free will allows us to say "Yes" or "No," and we live our lives with that choice. The list of options does not include "maybe, tomorrow, or someday." If we don't say, "Yes," the effort to postpone Him makes the answer "No."

Many years ago, I made a conscious decision and responded to God. I told Him that at the end of my life I did not want to have any regrets. For me, I have never regretted saying "Yes" to His invitation. While I highly recommend it, my goal is not to sway or coerce. You have your own free will. Your choice, your decision.

> "Listen! I am standing at the door, knocking;
> if you hear my voice and open the door,
> I will come in and eat with you, and you with me."
> Revelation 3:20

On Ingratitude and Good Manners

ingratitude: n. A lack or absence of gratitude; thanklessness.

manners: plural n. Ways of behaving toward people, esp. ways that are socially correct and show respect for their comfort and their feelings.

Leprosy, an infection caused by slow-growing bacteria, mainly affects the skin, peripheral nerves, and eyes. Untreated, the age-old disease can cause blindness, non-healing ulcers, and nose disfigurement, among other things.

During biblical times, leprosy was quite prevalent. However, no treatment existed. The afflicted, commonly viewed as accursed by God, were required to shout, "Unclean, unclean!" as a warning to those they might encounter while walking the countryside. Ostracized by their communities and families, they endured a difficult, heart-rending way of life.

While walking to Jerusalem, Jesus was met by ten lepers. His reputation for healing and performing miracles must have preceded Him, because the men cried out to Him for mercy. Jesus told them to go to the priests. While on their way, a miracle took place: All ten were healed. While the others continued on, one of them returned to Jesus to express his gratitude. The cleansed man fell at His feet, praising and thanking Him while giving glory to God.[8]

---

[8] Luke 17:15–18

Jesus freely healed ten lepers—not just one, but all ten of them. His gift affected and changed the rest of their lives by rescuing them from a lifelong curse. And yet, only one of the ten returned to thank Him for that gift. We can only speculate why the others exhibited ingratitude.

In a dream, that same response of ingratitude was doled out to one who bestowed generous favor on strangers. I still remember it and its message to this day:

Built high atop a solid rock edifice, the expansive mansion, a landmark in the city, could only be accessed by a trolley system. Well-designed and maintained, the trolley transported the inhabitants and their supplies as well as any who might visit.

The home resembled a castle, an unusual design in modern America. The new proprietor had recently completed a massive renovation of the entire building and sent out a blanket invitation to the locals to visit. Food would be served, and all were welcome to attend.

I knew the owner well. Our friendship went back decades, but I had not seen her in several years. As could be expected, parking at the base of the mountain was at a premium. Vehicles packed into every imaginable area as hordes of people clamored for a seat on the trolley to head up to their destination. I finally found a place to park my truck and joined the masses.

As I entered the home, the generous spread indicated my friend spared no expense. Large quantities of food filled the tables, available to all. Unlike some banquets, where food is measured out to the ounce per plate, guests could help themselves and eat until satisfied.

The crowd began to thin as people had their fill and headed back down the mountain. I did not intend to eat but to reconnect with my friend. Seeking her out, I found her seated, with her head bowed, sad and somber. "What's going on?" I asked. She then told me not a single person who had so freely eaten at her table said, "Thank you" as they left.

As I opened my eyes, I realized I'd had a dream, a powerful one. In the light of day, dreams often vaporize as details fade just out of reach. This one did not fall in that category.

So much of the current culture in my country, the United States of America, revolves around what "I want" or, even worse, "I deserve," with zero acknowledgment of the freely given gifts we already possess. Start with the fact all humankind enjoys the breath of life, a gift from our Creator. Often, people don't even acknowledge God's role in life and death until He removes that breath. Then, those left behind often strike out in anger because He did not ask their permission.

In addition, our way of life, even at its worst, ranks much higher than many others in the world. How many in our nation actually appreciate that? Ingratitude is an attitude, one that taints and poisons not only the one who possesses it but all who encounter that person. Flowing over into—and flooding—society, ingratitude quickly turns sweet waters bitter.

I had a dream. Yet that dream graphically illustrates reality.

As a parent, I freely give to my children. I do not give with the contingency of being told, "Thank you," but knowing they possess an attitude of gratitude fills my heart with joy. My Heavenly Father does not differ. He loves giving to His children and would withhold nothing from them. Even as Christ healed the nine who gave Him no acknowledgement, He asks for nothing in return. I feel, however, a simple "Thank you" is appropriate.

Gratitude and good manners cost the giver absolutely nothing. They are personal gifts only we can give.

May we give the One who loves us without measure appreciation and thanks for all He does for us, all He gives us. Be the one who returned to give glory to God for healing instead of one of the nine. At the very least, it's just good manners.

The Earth Is *Not* the Center of the Universe

Glorious weather set the stage for a wonderful day to spend in thought. Typically, January in my part of the world, the Willamette Valley floor in Oregon, wears a cloak of gray and grim, cold and dank. This past January, however, brought with it burgeoning evidence of spring. My quince shrub revealed early bright-red blooms, and brave daffodils showed their faces. Camellia bushes flashed their colors, and rhododendron everywhere were ready to explode into swaths of beauty. That week even set a record for warmth on a particular day in January, reaching 68 degrees.

My thoughts meandered while I worked in the sun, reveling in the bright, blue sky with its fluffy, puffy white clouds.

One of my first gardening clients in the area passed away quickly and unexpectedly. When given the harsh sentence of an aggressive, terminal condition, Dorothy (aka Dot) immediately responded, "Wonderful!" She knew the end of this life meant a step into the next one and met the journey wholeheartedly.

Dorothy's daughter asked me to clean up her garden—the task for the day. In times past, I could feel her presence as I fully expected the diminutive sprite-of-a-woman to wander out the front door, her face lighting up with a broad smile as she greeted me. This time felt different. I knew more important things occupied her time, and the stash of oak leaves that buried the landscape did not concern her in the least.

I spotted the property line marker as soon as I began. *If Dorothy were still alive,* I thought, *she would be thrilled and relieved.* She had been unable to find the bright orange marker for quite some time, which provoked a great deal of frustration and mental anguish. And yet that dilemma does not matter a whit to her now.

The necessity for property markers, which indicate boundaries, exists in the material, physical world of real estate. In God's realm, they have no relevance. He created our world and all the universe. He gives us residency.

My thoughts continued to wander. I remembered watching a video of a man who dropped dead yet fully recovered. A soft-spoken gentleman, he told of his experiences—conversing with God, the things he saw, and his life upon returning to his body.

Fortunate is the man or woman who knows our world does not revolve around the governments of the world and their heads. As important as any one leader or group feels they might be, their insignificance shouts in comparison to God.

Fortunate is the one who knows the possessions of this life do not transfer into the next one. Financial portfolios with investments and real estate; bank statements; listings with "Who's Who"; political, religious, scientific, financial, or educational credentials; awards in any given industry, by any group of people—none of them have any value in the next realm. No 401(k) will ever be rolled over into eternity. Nothing of this world can be used in the next, neither power nor material wealth.

The greatest fortune extends to those who know we live in a spiritual world—God's world.

Fortunate are those who know these truths.

We live in an information age, an age of electronics. We can hear about and see virtually everything worldwide *as* it happens, including natural disasters, wars, and elections. Still, this earth and life on this earth are not the center of the universe.

And so my mind roamed. I do not know where God dwells. However, as I cleaned up the oak leaves in Dorothy's garden, I realized *He* is the center of the universe. As Creator of all, He owns it all. Everything in this world, universe, and beyond revolves around Him, wherever that may be. That is where *I* want to be.

Now, as I sit looking out my window, hallmark fog has enveloped the scenery. I wrapped myself in a blanket to ward off the chill. When I lived at the coast, the old-timers used a term to describe the weather we've had the past few days. They called it a "false spring."

The next time I head off to work, I'll make sure to don an extra layer of clothing. The "false spring" has come and gone. And the thoughts will continue.

*"Do not lay up for yourselves treasures on earth,
where moth and rust destroy
and where thieves break in and steal;
but lay up for yourselves treasures in heaven,
where neither moth nor rust destroys
and where thieves do not break in and steal.
For where your treasure is, there will your heart be also."*
Matthew 6:19–21 NKJV

On Being Homogenized

homogenous: adj. Of the same kind; alike, similar. Having the same composition throughout; of uniform makeup.

We, the citizens of the United States of America, illustrate that of a nation living out a paradox. My nation can no longer tout unity. Division reigns. Yet a push to eliminate voices that counter a prescribed and predetermined thought pattern has come to the forefront. (Isn't that called censorship?) In other words, those in power want our nation's citizens to become homogenized. One can earn the label of phobic, racist, terrorist, or the next popular catch phrase that will become a trendsetter by simply dissenting, disagreeing, or expressing an opinion contrary to the accepted narrative.

Conforming, becoming homogenous, contradicts the fact that God created us as individuals. He gave each of us the right to be our own person, which includes having personal thoughts, opinions, and perspectives. No one has the license to discount them because they don't like them or disagree. Neither does any other human have the authority to label, silence, or require I become part of the mix and become "homogenized."

I am the daughter of a farmer who raised milk cows. I know that raw milk separates and the cream rises to the top. Milk that undergoes high pressure becomes homogenized milk. The process involves dispersing the fat, so no identifiable separation remains.

An enormous amount of pressure has been placed on those of us who refuse to conform. I say, "Leave that process for milk. I am my own person."

Be true to yourself before God and watch the cream rise. That's where you will find the quality product, the high-dollar stuff. Ask any dairyman who gets paid by the amount of butterfat in the milk his cows produce.

Separation reveals the superior nature of not only milk but people as well. Homogenization obliterates it.

Step out from the world. You belong to God.

> *"Come out from among them, and be separate," says the Lord.*
> *"... I will be a Father to you, and you shall be My sons and daughters, says the LORD Almighty."*
> 2 Corinthians 6:17–18 NKJV

Not of this World

of: prep. Used as a function word to indicate belonging or a possessive relationship.

I pulled up to the stop sign behind the red beast of a truck. The small size of the decal and the font's ornate feature made the words on its back window difficult to read. I finally figured it out while we both waited: *Not of this World*. The message resonated with me.

After my turn at the stop sign, it appeared we were taking the same route. I continued following the truck as I mulled over the truth of that window decal.

Utter and complete chaos currently rules the world and everything in it. The United States of America has become a people divided, even brother against brother, as various factions attempt to destroy the very fabric of this nation. Rampant crime plagues every corner of our country, with a complete disregard for the rule of law on every level, from those in elected positions of power down to ordinary citizens.

Riots disrupt tranquil peace in Europe. Discontent riddles parts of South America, and Central America does not differ. A global pandemic brought about mandates and lockdowns, robbing its citizenry of the freedom to live their ordinary, daily lives.

Countries controlled by dictators tout their military power. Still others have expressed the desire and intention to annihilate all who disagree with their religious beliefs, those they label "infidels." America has been dragged into an overseas war, one with the real potential of nuclear action.

In my own neighborhood, a local citizen was shot and killed in front of a middle school one hundred yards away from my front door. This, after he drew his own gun and fired at a police officer. I heard the gunfire and screams as I sat at my computer.

Recent legislation and its celebrations sicken me . . . legislation that allows the abortion of an unborn infant in the final stages of pregnancy, from twenty-four weeks to birth.

Evil hides behind the description of good. Good has inaccurately been labeled evil. Lies allege to be truth. Truth is called a lie. Morality and justice are only words.

We live in an environment filled with rampant and pervasive worldwide division, hatred, and anger.

How does one find peace amid such turbulence? God compels us to look to Him.

I do not belong to this world. I am *in* it but not *of* it. Simply expressed, I belong to my Creator and His Kingdom.

Think in terms of a family, a group of people, a citizenship who share the same experiences, goals, or ideals. Not only does a person belong with them, but one fits there. I do not fit in this world.

My little blue truck seemed to be stalking the red beast as I followed. I wanted to meet the driver and thank them for the message posted in their window. The truck turned onto a gravel road leading into an industrial parking lot, where the driver parked. I stopped my truck, got out, and approached her. "What does the sticker in your window say?"

She repeated what I already knew then asked, "Are you 'not of this world' too?" Nodding, I thanked her for the reminder to focus on God and not the prevalent, current insanity.

I do not know her name. She doesn't know mine. But we share a like mind, and in that we connected.

God reminded me He specializes in choreography as He brings His people together in unusual, random, and unexpected ways. I am part of a larger picture playing out, one not of this world. So are others, including the woman with the decal in her truck window. And that plan is an eternal one, the Kingdom of God.

You just never know what the day is going to bring.

Do not be conformed to this world,
but be transformed by the renewing of your mind.
Romans 12:2 NKJV

II
Life and the Living of It

Life. We have all been given one.
Use yours wisely. Live it well.
Don't squander your precious gift from God.

The Faint of Heart

faint of heart: lacking the courage to face something difficult or dangerous.

It is official. The dates have been confirmed, reservations made, plane tickets purchased, and seats assigned, ones with "extra leg room, please." The three-week-long trip to Scotland can no longer be viewed as a "someday" dream or a possibility but a reality.

Visiting Scotland is not for the faint of heart, I thought. *It's not all that different from living life with God.*

The small country of Scotland occupies the northern third of an island, sharing a sixty-mile-long land border with England on the southeast. Large bodies of water, along with nearly 800 islands, surround its remaining area: the Atlantic Ocean to the north and west, the North Sea to the northeast, and the Irish Sea to the south. Moving Atlantic depressions bring strong winds continuously throughout the year, earning it the title of "The Windiest Country in Europe." Those winds can be bitter and biting, the kind that chill to the very marrow of both visitor and inhabitant.

Its temperate climate tends to be changeable but not extreme. With the sun shining just over 25 percent of the time, however, gray and gloomy weather often casts a pall across the land.

Travel agents never advertise Scotland as a "warm and sunny" destination. A visitor must come prepared for inclement weather with the possibility—even the probability—of experiencing bone-chilling rain and/or wind.

Why, then, would anyone want to deal with that?

Because the experience is so worth it.

As a sixteen-year-old in the summer of 1961, I found myself living with a family in sheep-farming country in East Lothian, Scotland, forty-seven miles east of Edinburgh.

Coming from a small town and a sheltered environment, I traveled cross-country by train with other exchange students from Oregon to New York City before flying to Britain. I rode solo, by rail, on the final leg from London to Edinburgh. The experience of that summer changed my life.

Initially, a case of homesickness of grand proportions hit me so hard I became physically ill. In a time predating electronic communication, contact with family and friends at home took place solely via letters, now known as "snail mail." All alone in a very large world, I had no one to rely on but God. It was just God and me.

Fifty-eight years later, my eldest daughter and grandgirl will go with me as I return to visit the siblings of my Scottish family and their families.

Ancient history fills the country of Scotland. Castles from centuries ago reveal themselves as one drives around a bend in the road. Nature's rich and vibrant colors abound in its spectacular scenery. From farmlands to majestic mountains, with water everywhere, pristine beauty compensates for the country's diminutive size. The Scots are warm, friendly, and outgoing. The lilt of their accent on my native tongue of

English reminds me of listening to music. The sound of bagpipes causes my soul to melt.

Scotland and its people are forever a part of my being. I am possessed—from the time I first stepped off the train and my host family greeted me all those years ago.

I can say the same of God. He possessed me.

I vividly remember approaching the minister as he greeted parishioners leaving church at the end of a Sunday morning service, a tiny five-year-old girl standing next to a grown man. As he acknowledged my presence, I quietly said, "I want to go to heaven."

The journey began.

Living life with God is also not for the faint of heart. He does not change to live with us. We must be changed to live with Him.

Many speak of living life *for* God. Living life *with* Him is a completely different matter. When one lives *for* God, that often means having a personal project, idea, or plan, enacting it and bringing it about, then asking Him to bless it—the efforts of self.

Living *with* God means giving up my life and desires and allowing Him to have free rein. He requires total commitment—nothing more, nothing less. That demand flies in the face of everything within the being and nature of humankind, which probably explains why so few can pledge to walk the narrow path, the one leading to life.

Why, then, would anyone want to do that?

God created me from His perfect blueprint. His every action comes from a base of love and a desire for friendship. He knows me better than I know myself, and He wants only the best for me. Living life with God means living life where it really matters, in the eternal — the long-term rather than the short-term.

A constant, steadfast Companion, He walks me through the worst of times, the hardest of times, and shares in the best of times. I turn to Him daily, seeking guidance, wisdom, strength, forgiveness, and healing.

In short, He is worth it.

And that explains why I feel visiting Scotland and living life with God don't differ much from one another: They both begin with an intense desire for personal experience. Each requires determination and commitment to follow through and not be dissuaded if difficult circumstances arise. For a Scottish tourist, the weather can present a harsh deterrent. From a spiritual viewpoint, living with God is solitary, often with great demands. The road leading to life can be arduous.

But they do differ: My visit to Scotland ends after three weeks. Living life with God lasts two lifetimes — this one *and* the next to come.

As you continue reading these "sermons," may a seed be planted within you, the reader, one that encourages you to seek Him for yourself.

He *is* so worth it.

> *"Enter through the narrow gate,*
> *for the gate is wide and the road is easy*
> *that leads to destruction, and there are many who take it.*
> *For the gate is narrow and the road is hard*
> *that leads to life, and there are few who find it."*
> Matthew 7:13–14

For Your Eyes Only

If I had to sum it all up in a word, that word would be *horrible*. While I can state with certainty many things in life are much more difficult, the Sunday my grandgirls received the news they had to tell their family pet "goodbye" turned out to be even more terrible than I feared.

My daughter and son-in-law asked me to stay with the girls while they took Tank, the family's endearing lab, to the veterinarian to be put to sleep. The time had come. At the age of fourteen, cataracts diminished his vision. When I came through the front door, he hadn't heard me since his hearing had failed as well. Arthritis in his back hips made it increasingly difficult for him to carry his massive body and to navigate the steps outside. Developing tumors compromised him, and, even though he ate, visible bones outlined his once-staunch, vigorous frame.

For months, Tank's deteriorating physical condition could not be denied. The family openly discussed the inevitability of the situation. They all knew the end of his lifespan waited "just around the corner." Still, as often happens in many areas of life, reality presents a different story. The horrible shock and awful surprise resembled a rug being pulled out from underneath the feet of my grandgirls.

Mom and Dad gave them as much time as they needed to process the information. The girls hugged Tank, covering his body with theirs. Lying on the floor next to him, talking to him and petting him, the living room was filled with grief and gut-wrenching, heartbreaking sobs. They were ten and twelve. He had been part of their lives since their births. How does one let go of a best friend and companion?

A thought quietly entered my mind, and I shared it with the family. I suggested each girl write a letter to Tank, their "forever" buddy. In the letter they could tell him everything they wanted to say, all the things they wanted him to know and hear.

So, after their parents left for the vet office with Tank in tow, my grandgirls sat down at the table with pens and paper. Their crying subsided as they began to write, expressing their feelings and thoughts. I told them they were writing personal feelings and that they could hide the letter away forever, shared with no one if they chose.

"That was helpful," the little one said, as she folded up her letter and left to tuck it in her memory box. The older one agreed as she placed hers in a small baggie along with some of her pup's fur.

I am a proponent of this kind of writing. It cannot be called "writing a journal." Journals typically detail daily events. This entails venting, emptying and unloading from a person's inner depths. Call the process cleansing and cleaning out, if you will. Though no scientific data may exist giving support, my experience and conviction verify that something positive happens when one voices in such a manner, transferring from within to paper. After all, doesn't the essence of poetry, music, and composition come from that basis?

Many years ago, darkness filled my world. In my state of aloneness, I questioned all I once believed to be true. I knew and understood hopelessness and dreaded the beginnings of yet another day.

I began writing. Simply writing everything I thought, everything I felt. I began pouring out my doubts, questions, and frustrations onto the paper. And all the anger I felt toward a God whom I was certain had not heard my prayers. I *knew* He cared nothing about me.

I have no idea how long this continued, but the sessions covered quite a lengthy period. Despondent, filled with negative thoughts, troubled over my life and the way I lived it, I remember sitting at the kitchen table, filling page after page. Punctuation, grammar, and form be damned, I just wrote and wrote and wrote while pouring out all I felt and thought.

I reached a point when I finished, though I didn't realize it then. I did not complete a final chapter or write a *finale*. The need to vent simply no longer existed. Just as one does not dig through a garbage can, I had no desire to reread all I had released. I threw it all in the trash. No one ever read the writings. Only God and I even knew of their existence.

By that time, a healing process had begun. Physical wounds cannot heal with the presence of infection. Our inner beings respond the same way. Negatives breed toxicity and must be removed. Personally speaking, that occurred when I wrote letters to God. It began with a first step, one of being honest and real — with myself and with Him. When I started writing the opening sentence I never expected to end up at His doorstep. But I did.

For those of you in a chronic set of circumstances, behavior, or memories that haunt, daunt, or taunt you, robbing you of joy and peace in your life and the living of it, may I offer a suggestion? Find a quiet place, a piece of paper, and pen or pencil, and begin writing any thoughts that come to your mind.

Talking with a friend or even a professional has value and merit. However, I feel no substitute exists for pencil and paper, baring one's soul in black-and-white as you sweep out the recesses, crevices, and corners of your mind. Try it. You might be surprised at the outcome. It costs nothing, and, for me, it became one of the most valuable experiences of my life.

Remember, it is for your eyes only.

On Doing Dishes by Hand

I remembered I'd run the dishwasher the night before when I reached for a spoon in the drawer and found only two clean ones remaining. I needed to empty it, a task I often grumble about. *It just takes so long*—even though it never takes more than a few minutes to return the clean dishes to the cupboards and drawers.

Recently, I've been thinking about dishwashers, washing dishes, and a time, for the most part, observed in a rearview mirror.

As a youngster growing up, Mom expected me to dry the dishes she washed and rinsed. She never allowed them to air dry—God forbid! So, every night after supper, my mother and I could be found at the kitchen sink as she washed and I dried—and mother and daughter talked.

The towels used to dry the dishes had been designated specifically for that purpose. Made of a heavy cotton that absorbed the water before becoming sopping wet, they received treatment reserved for the finest of linens. The care taken to keep them stain-free cannot be exaggerated. The unused ones lay ironed, placed in a drawer. Several of them wore hand-embroidered embellishments, some with days of the week, others with a variety of figures.

My mother never had a dishwasher. In part, her closet-sized kitchen might have made that impossible. However, I doubt she would have agreed to such an appliance even if she had room.

I cherish the memories of those times at the kitchen sink when Mom and I talked. I don't remember most of our conversations, but I do remember she commented more than once, "Things could be worse." That response never made me feel better. While I didn't say it out loud, I countered with an immature, childish thought: *Things could be better too.*

I am quite certain she did a lot of listening to her daughter, the talker. Her quiet, soft-spoken manner contrasted sharply with mine. Occasionally she would ask, "Are you nice to everyone at school?" She knew her daughter well.

During high school, she helped me study Latin verb conjugations, English vocabulary words, or facts for a test. She propped up the study sheet in the kitchen window so she could review it with me while she washed.

When holidays or company came, stacking used dishes in the sink and leaving them dirty never received any consideration. Women of all ages dealt with them immediately, filling the small kitchen as they washed, dried, and put dishes away. Those were good times, filled with family and friendship, laughter, and chatter. They remain in my memory with fondness.

I must have carried those memories and experiences forward into my own life, as I resisted the use of a dishwasher myself for quite a while. I found the time spent cleaning up the kitchen, washing and drying the dishes, then putting them away therapeutic — my quiet time alone. There aren't a whole lot of quarrels within a family as to who gets to help with the dishes, and I opted to do them myself.

I am an advocate for spending time alone with oneself and one's thoughts. I still have memories of sinking my hands into the hot, soapy water, deep in thought as I bared my soul—not to my mother, but to my Creator.

As my family expanded to four children, I consented to using a dishwasher. My own children did not grow up as I did, sharing time at the kitchen sink after a meal. Things often happen like that as methods of accomplishing tasks fall away from one generation to the next, replaced by a completely different technique or approach. Some would call that progress.

We live in a culture that operates at breakneck speed, where much of life has an instantaneous feature available. Some positives exist in this, such as being able to share in my grandgirl's first dance via text and pictures. However, with a cell phone often readily available, a sacrifice has taken place—that of quiet solitude.

I still believe time spent alone remains invaluable. While I don't do dishes by hand anymore, that doesn't keep me from going to that place of reflection within.

As with all things in life, finding time alone consists of personal and individual choices. Many daily activities, such as walking, gardening, organizing drawers or cupboards, cleaning out a garage, or driving can be done with no outside distraction. A time of peace and quiet may be difficult to find in a busy life but *can* be made available and had by all.

I stand by my conviction that time alone with one's thoughts before God serves as one of the greatest investments that can be made in life. Search, seek, question, and reflect in true, honest thought. No method exists to measure its value. It *is*, however, time well spent.

Be still, and know that I am God!
Psalm 46:10

Being Schooled by a Child

school: v. To educate, teach, or train (often, but not necessarily, in a school).

Many people feel children should be viewed as helpless little creatures with no insight into life or how to live it. They assume that, as adults, only *they* hold the keys to knowledge, experience, and understanding—and the "littles" fill the role as pupils.

No one should question the idea that our children need examples and role models, guidance, and support. However, as adults, we *can* learn a great deal from *them*.

I picked up the grandgirls from school, and we went straight to a dental appointment. As I drove, I caught up on the lives of a fourth- and a sixth-grader. The conversations always have a lot of giggles interspersed, and I didn't allow the radio to be turned on. I wanted to visit with them.

When we arrived at the office, they took their homework in with them to work on while waiting. "Do you know how to do exponents, Gram Gram?" asked the older one. I gulped, feigning bravado.

"Well, let's look," I said. Fortunately, enough math from long ago had remained in my brain to be of help, and we worked on it together. Assignment completed.

The little one was next: "I'm going to need some help, Gram Gram. Will you help me?"

"Of course." She began working, and it was quickly apparent she really needed no help at all. With her legs propped up on an ottoman and her notebook in her lap, she tackled the assignment, that of renaming numbers in a variety of ways.

She peered up at me as she got to the bottom of the page. Very quietly, as though she needed to tell me a secret, she said, "We had a test, and we had to do this same kind of work. When I finished, I wrote a little note to my teacher: 'Thank you for teaching me these strategies.' There was some space left on the page, so I just wrote it."

To say I was dumbfounded would be an understatement. I can only imagine how her teacher felt. What nine-year-old child even thinks that way? This one does. And the beauty of it: She has no idea her approach to people and life can only be called atypical.

She is simply being herself. This *is* who and what she is.

The grandgirl I call "the little pit bull" took me to school yesterday. This time she taught me the value of expressing appreciation and thanks. But then she often schools me on other aspects of living a virtuous life as well.

Some of life's greatest lessons can be learned at the hand of, or from the mouths of, children. Listen. Pay attention. Give them time and respect. The world will be a better place.

And a little child shall lead them.
Isaiah 11:6

Flex and Flow

flex: n. Flexibility, pliancy. v. To bend something.

flow: n. Smoothness or continuity. v. To move as a fluid from one position to another.

The weather has a habit of not cooperating with my to-do list. At all! I am fully aware the weatherman predicted rain. However, I go into denial with any forecast until evidence proves me wrong. When I see raindrops splatting in puddles outside my front window, I cannot refute the prognostication. Then, and only then, do I concede. Once again, the weatherman wins.

I have been beating my head against a wall for days now, figuratively speaking. The gardening work, with spring's expansion of growth, has come on all at once. I still haven't addressed my Sunday mow jobs. It rained then as well. I had those scheduled for today.

I usually keep my Thursdays free, and I'd planned on accomplishing so much! The prospects of that happening look pretty "iffy" at this point.

Life consists of all sorts of variables, curve balls that come in unexpectedly. As a self-employed gardener, the weather often creates that situation for me.

The unplanned can come in the form of health issues, a mechanical breakdown in the family car, the need to replace an appliance, or home repairs. A delay in an airline flight or an appointment that takes longer than expected can easily alter daily schedules.

The "thorns in the side" have no end in life. Many times our lives don't go as planned, and the saying "If you don't bend, you break" expresses a great truth.

Mentally, I wrestle with this sort of day. I fight giving in to the reality that I have been grounded. You can find me constantly peering outside to see if the rain has subsided, providing a window of opportunity for outdoor work. I have no peace.

This morning, however, I remembered a principle prescribed to me many years ago, that of flexing and flowing, dancing with God as I allow Him to lead.

Flex and flow go hand in hand, one following the other. I am not in charge of my life, nor do I control it. That belongs to another. Today seems like a good day to practice what I preach, the concept of flexing and flowing with God.

A friend recently asked if I ever just "veg and nap." As I watched the rain come down a bit ago, it occurred to me today might be a good day to experience that. I started by lighting candles. Surely that will set the tone for relaxing. When it comes to the work, it certainly isn't going anywhere.

This much I know: When I flex and flow, my life takes on a positive tone. When I fight and resist the circumstances in my life, a sour, negative attitude develops. Flowing *with* God propels one forward. Struggling against His Spirit creates friction and resistance. The choice and decision belong to me.

On Change

change: n. The process of becoming something different.

The move out of an apartment into a duplex provided just cause for celebration. In addition to having a large yard of my own, I had new neighbors—my family, who lived in the adjacent unit.

My son-in-law removed several slats in the fence between the two backyards to make an opening, a pass-through from their yard into mine. My grandgirls, daughter, son-in-law, and I then had just a short trek from back door to back door.

An established routine developed. First, I heard knocking. Then, as I peeked through the window, two little girls peered back. Standing on the step, they waited to be invited in. Having my family living next door was a welcome part of my life and world for several years, one which brought me great joy.

When they moved into a larger home, my son-in-law replaced the slats, closing the opening. I had no idea how much that one simple change would impact me. I cannot tell you the countless number of times I headed next door, only to run into that boarded-up fence. Nor can I express the emotions that stirred within every time it happened.

The closed-off opening made a statement of a much larger whole. Life changed when my family moved and no longer lived next door. I had no knowledge or awareness of their daily activities. They did not share *my* everyday life and routine.

There is change. And then there is change. We experience outer, physical change daily, played out in nature, in our surroundings, and in life's circumstances. One could call it a fact of life. The other is personal in nature, taking place within, as the choices and decisions we make affect the kind of people we become and the ensuing direction of our lives.

Physical change can provide both an impetus and opportunity for personal growth and development. One needs only look at the stagnancy of standing water to draw a graphic picture of the importance of personal improvement.

Change might take place in our environment, but that doesn't necessarily mean personal changes result. A friend and I talked recently. She commented, "I have moved, and everything is different in my physical world. Yet nothing within me has changed. I am still the same. My life is too." She recognized and acknowledged the need to be transformed within, in the inner being, as one of great importance.

The converse is true as well. Everything might physically remain the same, but I am able to become a different, better person. I can change and *be* changed.

A work from the inside out is preferable and results in true change. It is where you find yourself with nary a ruffled feather when in times past temper and anger would have flared; where patience, tolerance, and understanding replace impatience and intolerance. True change: when you find yourself listening, really listening, instead of needing to dominate or to be heard, where you have inner peace instead of turmoil.

This type of personal change has no monetary price tag. Self-effort does not bring it about and can only be classed as a gift from God. Change like this doesn't necessarily come easily and often comes at a price, that of giving up self and one's own way. It does, however, bring with it evidence of life with continuing personal development and growth.

My family no longer lives next door where I see them daily. The fence without an opening is part of my everyday life. I have made the adjustment.

I have a goal, a desire. I want to become the person God had in mind when He created me. That cannot happen on my own but only at His hand. For me, this is change that truly matters.

On Stamina

stamina: n. The energy and strength for continuing to do something over a long period of time; power of sustained exertion, or resistance to hardship, illness, etc.

"You certainly have stamina," my client said as he walked by. I laughed. You know, the nervous laugh that spills out when you've been given a compliment and find yourself rendered speechless.

The task at hand consisted of cleaning up the iris beds. New growth had already started to raise its head, so the job required cutting back spent vegetation and hauling it off. At one thousand feet above the valley floor, the nights were cold in the garden where I worked. The days bore warmth, though. Getting outside and accomplishing some physical work always feels productive.

Even so, I found the ground still frozen in the shade. I came prepared, wearing several layers of clothing, including double thicknesses of both gloves and socks. When my client expressed his observation, I had already been working about four hours, manually plowing through masses of still-frozen dead growth, cutting it back with my hand scythe.

While I responded audibly with nervous laughter, my mental reaction revealed confidence: *You should see my spiritual stamina.*

The laughter and ensuing thought set my mind in gear.

What does that word even mean? I had the concept and a general idea, but I could put nothing into an intelligible description. *Do I really have spiritual stamina? Or am I just deceiving myself with mental word games and false confidence?*

Stamina manifests itself like a heartbeat, a solid, silent force that brings about fulfillment and completion. The presence of stamina does not draw attention; you'll never find it to be showy or flashy.

As with all things in life, those areas where you'll find stamina revealed have as much uniqueness as the ones exhibiting it. I feel stamina exposes resolve, endurance, and true grit. They go hand in hand.

One of my daughters ran a 50K trail race. I told a friend of the accomplishment, and he responded, "You mean 5K?"

"No, 50K."

She traversed a trail that carried her thirty-two miles and took seven hours and forty-five minutes. The race ended with a mile-long vertical climb up steps. *That* takes stamina. This same daughter has run six marathons, including one in Chicago, and more half-marathons than she can count.

I know another woman, one in her late seventies, who personifies stamina, which manifested in different circumstances. She spent this past year dealing with the kind of diagnosis everyone dreads, a rare, fast-growing cancer.

She endured two surgeries and a regimen of chemotherapy followed by radiation, resulting in loss of her hair, energy, and strength. I suspect her will to live was challenged as well. The life of this vibrant, active woman ground to a halt. She loves to walk and garden, but those activities shut down as she went through the process laid out for her.

As she forges ahead in a new year, I see her once again, striding down the sidewalk, a walking stick in her hand "just in case." Vegetables appear at my garage door as she shares her lush garden.

That is stamina.

How does one describe spiritual stamina? Spiritual stamina does not differ from physical stamina except it takes place in the spirit and results in a long-term, eternal outcome rather than short-term and earthly.

I believe when it comes to spiritual aspirations, God gives us exactly what we will settle for. If people prefer living in doubt, questioning, and unbelief, why should they be given anything above and beyond? If a relationship with God has no importance, then what would be the point of having that? If a person does not strive for truth and knowledge, the manifestation of love, wisdom, forgiveness, and peace, what value would these have for someone if God handed them over?

Spiritual stamina comes into play, however, for those with lofty spiritual desires. People with spiritual fortitude will never give up in their quest for a walk with God. They will be driven by the goal of living a virtuous life and bringing honor to Him. Spiritual stamina becomes visible when nothing remains within, when no reserves remain to carry on. And yet they continue seeking, asking, and digging in with all their heart, soul, and mind.

I possess grand, specific spiritual ambitions as I live life and deal with my Creator. After examining the meaning of that word, I have concluded and can announce: "Yes, I do have spiritual stamina." And back to where these thoughts began. I finished cleaning up the iris bed before I quit for the day. It's that stamina thing.

> *I have fought the good fight;*
> *I have finished the race;*
> *I have kept the faith.*
> 2 Timothy 4:7

On Caring

care: v. To be concerned about, have an interest in; to be mindful of.

care: n. Close attention; concern, responsibility; the object of watchful attention or anxiety.

"Thanks for checking in on me. I need that sometimes." The succinctness and directness of her response surprised me.

My twelve-year-old grandgirl had taken an opponent's knee to her thigh in a basketball game the day before. When it happened, I was focused on another part of the court. Turning back, I saw her on the floor, writhing in pain as she grabbed her leg. She's a tough one, not prone to drama, so I knew she wasn't pretending. I contacted her the next day, asking how the injury felt after Mom's and Dad's physical therapy and a night's rest. The simple inquiry touched her.

Caring brings with it a single stipulation—either you care or you don't. One cannot feign or fabricate caring. A person either feels genuine concern or none at all. Care is evidenced—and felt. Saying one cares does not prove, validate, or verify it either. "Words are cheap."

What does it mean to care, really care?

Caring entails paying attention to, and making note of, another person and the circumstances in their life. In essence, it means going beyond the involvement, concerns, and interests of self. Its base consists of putting thoughts of another's welfare ahead of "me."

Infants provide the perfect example of self-centeredness. By nature of their helplessness and inability to care for themselves, they care about no one *other* than themselves. They certainly have no concern about the sleep deprivation their parents experience. An infant couldn't care less whether or not they make a public spectacle because they are hungry or upset.

As children grow and develop, mentors guide and teach them, and they learn the lessons that cause them to understand the world does not revolve around them. They learn to care about other people besides themselves.

Caring about a fellow human being or the circumstances in others' lives costs the giver nothing. Even so, its importance and value can be quite substantial, and one should never underestimate its impact.

Recently, a friend experienced a difficult time. "You doing okay?" I asked.

"Yes. Your caring makes me feel better."

It takes so little to make a difference in others' days and lives. In addition, real, valid, and genuine concern boldly contrasts with behavior that shouts "counterfeit, superficial, and contrived."

The nature of humankind revolves around "me, myself, and I." Stepping outside that infantile box can become a rewarding and vital experience that provides personal benefits as well. When I share myself with others, my life is enriched.

Yes. Knowing someone cares does make a person feel better. Be that person. Care for others as God cares for you.

Those things money cannot buy are always the most valuable.

He cares for you.
1 Peter 5:7

On Living with a Threat

threat: n. A person or thing likely to cause damage or danger.

November snuck in through the back door unannounced. I turned my back, and our Indian summer disappeared. Wet days replaced warm, sunny ones with a cold, bone-penetrating chill.

Utility work was in progress down the street from my house. As I headed for my gardening job, traffic came to a halt, controlled by workers with stop/slow signs. *What an awful job,* I thought, considering the hours they spend standing in the wet, the cold, and the heat. The knowledge I have the freedom, as a self-employed person, to call it a day if the elements become too harsh heartened me. As I cranked up the heater in the truck, my work task for the day didn't seem so horrible.

Oh, how I would hate being a _____. For the life of me, for all the money in the world, I could not think of the job title given those workers with the signs. The threat I live with found its way into my mind, seeking a place to germinate and take root.

"Something is happening. I can feel it. I know it. I reach for a word, and it's gone. It's simply not there. Something horrible is happening in my brain." My friend, in her early fifties, expressed this repeatedly. I offered reassurances and, yet, at the same time, felt a foreboding all was *not* well. It turned out early Alzheimer's had begun taking over, a battle and struggle that went on for a long while. It ended in her death when she had only begun life as a senior citizen.

My mother lived with Alzheimer's for ten years before passing, so I know full well the horrors of that state. The phrase "a living funeral" describes the disorder aptly. When I talk about her condition, some, who have the perception I must see the handwriting on the wall as I await the passing down of a grisly family heirloom, ask, "Aren't you afraid?"

I spent the day raking fallen leaves, another product of November. I found myself raking, raking, raking, almost frantically, all the while trying to fill in that blank with the name of the occupation of those with the stop signs. At the same time, thoughts of my friend, and of my mother, consumed my mind, understanding exactly what she meant in describing the vaporization of a word.

Traffic controllers, security guards, crosswalk guards . . . No matter how hard I tried, I couldn't grab the elusive word from thin air. I became utterly distraught over my inability to identify something so familiar.

We all forget things. I maintained that, at the age of seventy, my mind could hold only a certain amount of information. Therefore, if it isn't genuinely important, it slips to the back of the memory file. While this didn't necessarily fall into that category, not being able to remember proved quite disconcerting. In addition, that Alzheimer's threat had seated itself firmly in my being.

Approaching my Heavenly Father, I heard myself say, *"I'm scared. I'm really scared."*

Going out on a proverbial limb, I will state that I feel living with a threat cannot be called a rare situation for people. We each have our own background and experiences. Many of those carry with them a genetic propensity or a family health history with serious ramifications. Perhaps one's family tree bears the scourge of cancer or diabetes. There may be heart conditions, mental illnesses, or addictive behavior among relatives. Obesity might stare full bore or, yes, Alzheimer's. The threats may present themselves in an insidious form or direct; occasional or frequent. They always target one's vulnerability and the emotional facet of self.

Living with a threat often means living life dodging a bullet while a guillotine hangs over one's head, never knowing what will trigger the release of the fatal blade nor when or where it will happen. I suspect you understand.

How *does* one live with a threat? I won't apply my approach to another. I can only relate how I deal with it.

In such circumstances I have learned I have the choice to either live in fear or live free from it. I refuse to allow the fear of being a victim of Alzheimer's to dominate and control me.

My mother's life is not mine. Therefore, my walk does not duplicate hers. I have chosen to live life with my focus on God, not the fear. Simplistic, unrealistic, naïve? Perhaps. But I can do nothing to control my future or my destiny. Only He can.

Flaggers! That is what they are called. Flaggers control traffic in road construction areas. I refused to search it out on the internet or ask someone. It did come to mind—after I stopped wrestling with trying to figure it out.

Some would say, "Thank God for minor miracles." It *is* a miracle; it isn't minor.

Thank You, God.

All I have asked you to do is to live your life.

*For God has not given us a spirit of fear,
but of power and of love and of a sound mind.*
2 Timothy 1:7 NKJV

How to Walk on Water

He said, "Come." So Peter got out of the boat,
started walking on the water, and came toward Jesus.
Matthew 14:29

Many of my generation, born in the middle of the last century, grew up attending Sunday school and church. Bible stories, gleaned from both the Old and New Testaments, were a large part of the curricula taught during our childhood. Those stories include one about a boy's lunch feeding a multitude. Another tells of Peter, a disciple of Jesus, and his encounter with waters deep.

Elisabeth and Mary, the mothers of John and Jesus, had a close relationship. They may have been cousins. While there is no way of knowing if their sons grew up together, as adults, John baptized Christ as He began His earthly ministry, publicly acknowledging Him as the Lamb of God.

John enraged Herodias, King Herod's wife, when he publicly admonished the king, informing him that marrying his sister-in-law was illegal. The king placed John in prison at her behest. At Herod's birthday celebration, she instructed her daughter, who danced for the king, to request John's head be given to her on a platter. Herod granted her wish.[9]

The news of John's death undoubtedly felt like a "gut

---

[9] Matthew 14:3–12

punch" to Jesus. Needing time alone, He left His disciples behind and went to find refuge in a boat out on the water.

Masses of people waited for Him to come back ashore. Filled with compassion, He pushed his personal grief aside, welcomed them, and spent the day healing and ministering to their needs.

As the long day came to an end, it became apparent the crowd had not brought food with them. A dilemma presented itself: They were hungry, but the deserted area had no villages nearby to supply nourishment for the crowd of five thousand men plus women and children.

A boy offered five small loaves of bread and two fish he had brought with him. (Isn't that just like a boy to make sure he took care of his stomach? Or a mother who knew her son well.) Jesus accepted his gift. He gave thanks for the food and blessed it. Surprisingly, the small offering multiplied beyond anyone's imagination. The throng ate until they were filled. Twelve baskets of leftovers provided evidence of the miracle. The crowd went back to their homes, satisfied both physically and spiritually.

As night fell, Jesus instructed His disciples to board the boat and head for the opposite shore. Feeling sorrow over hearing of John's death, He wanted to spend time alone with His Heavenly Father.

During the night, a severe storm developed while the disciples were still a great distance from land. Fierce winds and waves battered the boat about like a leaf, emphasizing their helplessness. The certain possibility of impending death caused fear to spread among them.

Early in the morning, Jesus appeared, walking on the sea toward them. Thinking He was a ghost, they became even more afraid. He tried to reassure them: "Take heart, it is I; do not be afraid."

Peter was not convinced. He asked for a sign of proof — that Jesus would call him to come out on the water.

"Come," Jesus said.

Clambering over the side, Peter began walking on the water toward Him. The raging winds caused the water around him to roil. A powerful gust struck with such intensity that Peter turned to look. When he did, he took his eyes off Jesus and promptly sank.

Jesus reached out His hand to lift Peter up and said, perhaps with a bit of humor in His voice and a smile on His face, "You of little faith, why did you doubt?"[10]

Many people classify Bible stories as fabricated tales of glory and intrigue that have duped the gullible and less educated. Those of faith disagree, believing in the stories' validity, reinforced by their own personal experiences with a living God.

The message could not be clearer: If I look at the storms surrounding me, I will sink every time. Every. Single. Time. And I do. However, knowing the truth and living it often become two different tales.

I have a lifelong friend who knows how to walk on water. She spent an entire year with severe physical problems. Excruciating joint pain took over her body, the kind that leaves no future other than life in a wheelchair. The suffering

---

[10] Matthew 14:13-33

remained relentless. After a year, the pain abated only to be replaced by blindness. It happened gradually, darkness taking over first one eye then the other.

I talk with her periodically. "How are you?" I ask.

Without fail, she responds, "Good." And she is.

I usually answer, "I'm okay" to the same question. There *are* times when I can say, "I'm good," but not with the same consistency as she does.

"You just have to look at the inner, not the outer," my friend says. She also acknowledges it *is* easier said than done. Staying focused on the inner and on God takes a lot of time and practice.

The world experienced an upheaval, a literal turning upside-down of everything once viewed as "normal." COVID-19, the 2020 pandemic, and the ramifications of it, took on the trappings of a giant sinkhole that continued growing, its center a vortex that would suck a person down if we allow it. The political landscape portends fulfillment of biblical prophecies. What does it all mean?

Lying in bed one restless night, I contemplated the long-term effects of the pandemic lockdown on my grandgirls, the push of government toward a one-world system called the New World Order, and every other detail and worry I could conjure up. This state forms the perfect picture of looking at the outer, the storm with the wind and the waves, which is the opposite of faith and trust.

I cried out to my Heavenly Father, a familiar plea when I mentally spin off into oblivion. I do not know how, when, or even why, but He always takes me to a better place, one of calm water.

How *do* you walk on water? Our walks with God are individual and personal. I personify Peter in the raw. I doubt. God responds. I look around at the storms and flail about, sinking. Ever faithful, He reaches out and lifts me up.

This much I know: I revel in the times of inner peace and calm, fully realizing they happen because I am looking to Him—not at the storms and garbage whirling around me.

That is how and what it means to walk on water.

Just Keep Me Going

Thoughts filled my mind today about a situation in my life, one with no easy answers. I heard myself say, *"Just keep me going. Just keep me going."* Yes, I do spend a lot of time alone in my work as a gardener. But, no, I have not gone over the deep end from too much solitude. I often express this plea when dealing with difficult circumstances as I recognize the need to continue moving forward, one step at a time.

Many years ago, I was discussing a problem with a friend. "What do I do?" I asked, expecting a list of suggestions.

The answer: "Just keep going. What else can you do?" Place that Number One on the list of Last Thing I Wanted to Hear! Over the years, though, I have come to realize the wisdom proffered in that response.

We all share a common experience, either past or present and likely in the future, circumstances in our lives that pretty much buckle us at the knees. Sometimes we actually feel as though we won't survive and may seriously consider if we even want to. Life may "bottom out" to a point of simply existing, as though in a tunnel, with no light and no end in sight. Darkness envelops, compounded by having no measure of understanding.

At times, even everyday life, without a major calamity, feels like we need to "tread water" as fast as we can to keep from sinking. Those are the times when we want to curl up in a fetal position and quit. Life feels too hard. You can try, but in all honesty, the fetal position never accomplishes much.

In this journey called life, I have had more than my fair share of times when I dug my heels in and refused to budge. In that state, progress comes to a standstill. Spinning on a hamster wheel creates an environment where attitudes sour and life stagnates. The scenery remains the same while daily living becomes a rut of repetition and drudgery, with no change. This kind of environment creates a breeding ground for other negatives to enter and thrive. A door opens, and in comes fear, bringing with it doubt and confusion. This condition can only be described as the antithesis of living.

This brings me back to the sage advice. Each of us has our own particular path, a very specific, individualized walk that is ours and ours alone. Just keep going.

How *do* you do that? To begin with, you can only take the steps right in front of you. But take them, you must. Other steps will follow.

For those times when I need to be pushed along, nudged from behind, and never allowed to stay in one place, my prayer is: *"Just keep me going."* The result has been a richer, fuller life than I could have imagined. And I have a much better view than when I'm stuck in a rut along the side of the road.

Just keep going.

On an Anniversary

anniversary: n. A day that is an exact number of years (to the day) since a given significant event.

I noticed my socks had holes in the heels. I need some new ones, I thought. If I had been thinking, I would have asked for some for Christmas.

The heels on my Smartwool socks have worn through, evidence of considerable use. I have been blessed with proverbial "cold feet." During the winter in particular, my warm socks remain a mainstay of daily life. I live in them, donning them as soon as I crawl out of bed.

Today is December 18. This singular pair of socks, though now revealing signs of wear, remains a constant reminder of that day a year ago.

Several members of my family and I went to Idaho for an early Christmas with the branch on the family tree who lives there. The girls in my family love to shop, so a group of us decided to explore downtown Boise wearing its full holiday display. All ten of us, two carloads worth, spread out as we trekked along, checking out the local stores. When I discovered a store that carried Smartwool socks, I knew God smiled down upon me. I had worn a previously gifted pair until they had no life left in them, and finding a store that sold them made me giddy. I completed my purchase, *my shopping needs fulfilled*.

It was cold, typical of Idaho in December. As I walked along, I stuck my hands in my coat pockets. The light at the crosswalk announced I had nine seconds to cross. As I rushed to beat the signal, the lugged sole on my Ugg boots caught on the pavement. I fell with such force that a daughter walking along behind me thought a gun had taken me down.

Most milestone events escape my memory, such as anniversaries, birthdays, dates of the passing of loved ones. I know the dates of my children's births and those of my grandchildren, and that's about it. I do remember this particular day, though, and I certainly won't forget the experience.

One year has passed. That year included one broken jaw and a seven-week-long liquid diet due to restrictive bands holding the jaw in place, one tooth broken off, five replacement crowns, an injured finger (note to self: do not walk on uneven surfaces with your hands in your pockets), a fat lip, and a scuffed knee, but not a single stitch.

As a much younger person, I had a "la la la" fairy-tale image of life with God. I viewed Him as not only a better deal than Santa Claus but a magical force as well, one that kept me safe and protected me in a bubble.

As He revealed Himself to me, I learned He doesn't keep me *from* difficult circumstances, but He does promise to walk through them *with* me.

I remember that first night after a visit to the emergency room. As I sat upright on a beanbag to alleviate pressure on the broken jaw, I asked God what I had done wrong. *Why?* I wanted to know why the "splat" happened. He did not answer.

Time heals. It also brings with it perspective. I discovered the truth: He does not operate in the way of humankind, that of good and bad, right or wrong.

As humans, we tend to categorize events in life as "good" or "bad." I learned some situations may be harder than others, but that doesn't make them bad. As for "right" or "wrong," God's only standard is righteousness. I can do nothing to meet that standard. Therefore, I *can* "do" nothing right.

I did not break my jaw because I had done something wrong or because I sinned. He knows my heart. I stand before him in purity, freed from the curse of sin because I acknowledge the sacrifice of His Son on my behalf. Every experience has a point and fulfills a purpose. All things happen at the hand of God.

One year later, I can attest to God's faithfulness. My Heavenly Father walked with me every step of the way, from the very beginning. I was going down face-first. At the last nanosecond, my head flipped to the side, and I landed on my jawbone instead. Given the force of impact, if my head had not turned, I could have suffered a broken neck, possibly rendering me paralyzed. At the very least, I would have dealt with massive facial injuries for the rest of my life. The potential for a life-altering event ended up as more of an inconvenience. That I broke only my jaw bears witness to the fact of His hand upon me.

Christmas is a week away. I'm not sure what the family has planned for Christmas dinner, but I guarantee everything will be better than what I had a year ago. I can't recall the exact content, but I do know I ingested the liquid "food" through a very small straw.

My son-in-law asked me to see if the oral surgeon could repeat the extreme banding procedure that stabilized the broken jaw. Since the restrictions made it quite impossible for me to talk, he said last year was the quietest Christmas the family has ever had.

Laughter *is* the best medicine.

God is good all the time. All the time, God is good. For me, this past year confirms that.

Yea, though I walk through the valley of the shadow of death,
I will fear no evil, for thou are with me.
Psalm 23:4 KJV

We know that all things work together for good
for those who love God,
who are called according to His purpose.
Romans 8:28

On Gliders and Thumpers and Other Differences

There are gliders in this world. And then there are thumpers. At least based on my experience. The two types could not be more opposite from one another than the South Pole is from the North Pole. Generally, gliders don't bother thumpers at all. However, the sounds made by a thumper often upset gliders.

Gliders enter a room quietly, barely making any sound, unless they wear high heels. On the other hand, you can hear a thumper approaching from quite a distance, with or without shoes, as the sound of footsteps reverberates through the air. On occasion, the solid force causes glassware in cupboards to rattle. The latter describes me to a "T." I openly admit and confess: "I am a thumper." I walk hard, a real understatement. In fact, "thud" would probably more accurately describe the sound I make than "thump."

I hadn't thought about that personal trait for quite a while. As a gardener, I don't make much noise walking behind a lawn mower and, living alone, am oblivious with no one to remind me when I'm loud. I took my shoes off today while cleaning a client's house. Because I land solidly on my heels first, the bare feet amplify the impact. I heard and observed the thump and the sound of rattling glassware. Memories of the chastisements from days gone by filled my mind. *"Why do you walk so hard? Can't you walk more softly? You're shaking the whole house. Try walking like a lady."* The comments from gliders were gone but not forgotten. I began processing the memories.

The unspoken message: Something was very wrong with me. *I* needed to change. I tried—more than once. The success rate never got past 0 percent, along with efforts to transform my curly hair to bone-straight, rid myself of a down-right stubborn streak, eliminate the procrastination factor, and change countless other traits and characteristics that make up the person I am.

It took a while to understand the way I walk shouldn't be categorized as right . . . or wrong. Everything about me, including my habits, differs from others. However, when one struggles with self-acceptance and self-confidence, the criticism becomes a monkey wrench thrown in that takes some time and sorting to figure out.

Another person's differences do not provide a just reason for rushing to judgment. Knee-jerk reactions often happen quickly, as people respond critically, without thinking. We all handle situations differently. For example, I drive in a manner different from other drivers on the road. How often does that upset the one in the car behind me as I cautiously wait for traffic to pass before turning onto a street? I have a habit of asking questions I already know the answer to. That creates its own frustrations in my family. And I haven't even begun to discuss differences in the way we think and view ethics, philosophy, politics, the environment, nature, and religion—just to name a few. We have no right to judge those differences in the lives of others as either right or wrong.

God created us as individual, human snowflakes. Therefore, we differ from one another.

Bias and an intolerance have developed in our society and our nation toward any who disagree with those in the position of power and control. A current, prevalent attitude exists: "We are right; therefore, you are wrong." Not so.

We think, believe, and act differently. But they are differences, not justification for division, rejection, or judgment. I differ in opinion and belief with many of my friends. That does not make me right and them wrong or vice versa. It means we possess individuality, with a right to our respective points of view.

My uniqueness, including that of being a thumper, and yours as well, came from God. God help us as a nation if we get to the point where its citizens and those in charge do not respect, expect, or allow differences. We are not clones and must not be treated as such. And for myself, I need to be very careful I don't come from a place of judgment when viewing others' differences, be they inner or outer.

I told a former client my "thumper" story, sharing the criticisms and harsh comments I've received over the years. "Did you know that is a good thing?" she asked. She went on to say her doctor told her walking with impact increases bone density. In fact, its value is based on the amount of impact. Who knew? Certainly not the gliders in my life. Nor I. It's all in how you look at things, isn't it?

May I treat others with the same level of respect I would like given to me—despite our differences.

> "Do not judge, so that you may not be judged.
> For the judgment you give
> will be the judgment you get."
> Matthew 7:1–2

On Time and the Giving of It

time: n. The inevitable progression into the future with the passing of present events into the past.

Time is a universal commodity given to every man, woman, and child living on the face of this earth. The amount of time allotted to each of us adds up to twenty-four hours in a day. Sixty minutes in an hour. Sixty seconds in a minute. No more. No less. Time can be called true equity.

Time takes on a different "feel" at various stages of life. For children, time often moves at a snail's pace as it seems they spend their life waiting, perhaps for a holiday or special event. Parents can't find enough of it to get everything done while meeting the demands of a family's rigorous schedule. Those of us living as senior citizens find ourselves dealing with the reality of time passing like a flash in the night. Many elderly folks live in a paradox. They have nothing but time on their hands as they live their days in solitude and loneliness. All the while, very little sand remains in their hourglass of life.

Whether consciously or unconsciously, we as humans categorize and prioritize our time. We schedule time for work, family, and leisure. We set aside time for events, activities, and vacation. And, God forbid if an interruption occurs—time for sleep. Most folks, however, never consider including another important category in their daily life. I call it "people" time.

When I give my time to another, I gift myself. I share "me." No one else can do that *but* me. Gifts can be purchased and delivered, but the gift of time carries no price tag. While volunteer work has a time and place, I am speaking of something different here.

"I'm busy now. I don't have time." How often do those words so easily slip off the tongues of family members or perhaps from one in a position of authority or a leadership role? Consider the message and the feeling it evokes: *You have interrupted me and my life. You do not matter enough for me to stop what I'm doing. Go away.*

We deliver that same message, though unspoken, as we plow through our daily lives making certain we do not interact with people we do not personally know. After all, we have things to do, people to see, and places to go. We'll never see these strangers again, so they don't really matter. Or do they?

Recently, I took a trip to visit a friend. I've known her for decades, and we have been close friends for the past several years. Neither of us has a sister. The term sister/friend fits perfectly.

After she picked me up, we stopped by the grocery store to get a few things. While waiting in line to check out, she quietly commented, "Just a minute. This lady needs some help." She saw what I hadn't. An elderly lady, so tiny a slight breeze could blow her away, struggled bagging her groceries. She had an over-sized container of detergent, far too heavy and bulky for her to handle. My friend stepped in, placed the items in sacks, and told her she would help get the groceries into her car.

"This is the last time I'm going to do this," the older woman commented. She shared she was in the process of moving into a facility where meals would be provided.

We finished checking out and headed to her car, loading the items in the back. The little lady chattered the whole time, talking about originally moving from Rhode Island and her current move. She was thrilled to be the recipient of the gift of time, evidenced by her gratitude and the smile on her face.

This kind of conduct isn't unusual for my friend. She gives time where and when needed as she gives of herself. And she does those things quietly, never seeking attention. Helping out a woman she doesn't know typifies the kind of person she is. I would call it her second nature—one without effort or pretense.

Recently, we talked about being available when called upon. Her comment has stuck with me: "You just have to make time. Loving the broken is loving God."

Though often unnoticed, therefore not acknowledged, the gift of time is a gift indeed. You will not hear a public service announcement with grand accolades. Bells and whistles won't fill the air, nor will any balloons be released into the sky. The gift of time consists of the act of being present, lending an ear, and providing companionship and help if needed.

Each of us is given a certain amount of time in life. Perhaps you have heard the charge to use your time wisely and make the most of it. The context of that admonition generally relates to an activity or a goal.

I ask you, however, to consider the value and importance of giving time as a gift. Give and share yourself. The world will be a better place.

> "And the king will answer them, 'Truly I tell you, just as you did it to one of the least of these brothers and sisters of mine, you did it to me.'"
> Matthew 25:40

On Stubbornness and Regret

stubborn: adj. Refusing to move or to change one's opinion; obstinate; firmly resisting; persistent in doing something.

regret: v. To feel sorry about (a thing that has or has not happened).

Every time I pulled up to the stoplight at the intersection of Chambers and 18th Street, thoughts about Deb filled me with deep remorse. More than once last fall, I chose to turn right and head homeward after a day of gardening work instead of going through the light to spend time with my friend.

I sat beside Deb in the doctor's small examination room at the local clinic when her physician issued the death sentence: duodenal cancer, a rare but fast-spreading cancer in the small intestine.

"This is only the second time I've seen it," he said. "The last time was twenty years ago when I was a resident."

In an attempt to comfort, I reached out to touch her. She pushed my hand away.

I had driven her to the appointment. A heavy, smothering weight filled the vehicle during the drive back to her house. I didn't handle any of the situation well. I had never been present at the delivery of a death sentence before. I probably tried too hard and said too much. I'm not sure. I still question myself and second-guess my responses.

Deb had no family other than an estranged brother. My heart went out to her. I offered myself and my services if she needed help of any kind.

I pulled back, *way* back, when she responded she felt I was smothering her. The statement stung. I felt stupid.

At that point, I dug my heels in.

I told her I wouldn't bother her anymore, but I reiterated my availability should she need help. I left it in her hands to reach out.

She called me once after that, asking me to drive her to an infusion appointment. When I got to her house, I found her vomiting, a side effect of the cancer. She had to cancel the procedure.

That turned out to be the last time I saw her. I knew she was on death's doorstep, but I made no effort to visit her. I held tightly onto my pride and perceived ill-treatment.

Many years ago, I asked God that, at the end of my life, I would have no regrets. Every time I came to that intersection, though, a companion showed up and rode in the truck with me—regret. I couldn't shake it. I sported a bruised ego and, along with it, I questioned my spiritual awareness and sensitivity.

I avoid confrontation, but I recently found myself in that place with someone I'm close to. The conversation ended in a collision with the comment directed at me: "Okay. I'm done."

Responding in the same way I did with my friend, I thought, *There you go then. I'm done too. It's in your hands.* Fortunately, my Heavenly Father entered my mind and heart. I knew I didn't want things to end up the way they had with Deb—too late.

I sent a message with the hope of reconciliation: "I love you. Always have. Always will." I received a positive response in return, one indicating love. Differences still remain, but at least the chasm has diminished. The situation *is* in God's hands.

God fills our lives with experiences designed by Him to teach, develop maturity, and make us more Christ-like. The next time I pull up to that intersection at Chambers and 18th, I won't be swamped with regret but filled with gratitude for a lesson learned.

Deb, my prayer for you has always been that you would see God and know His love for you. May you rest in peace.

My Rocking Chair Barometer and Worry

barometer: n. An instrument for measuring atmospheric pressure. Something that reflects changes in circumstances or opinions.

The rocking chair slowed from a frenetic pace to one of leisure. I then realized I had calmed down and entered a state of peace.

The rocker entered my home and my life more than twenty years ago. I bought it when I first became a grandmother. I wanted to have a rocking chair so I could cuddle and rock my grandbabies. It needed to be solid and well-made, able to withstand the rambunctious toddler stage as well. A worthwhile purchase, the chair has survived as a silent reminder of hours spent with five precious little girls, now young women.

I replaced the original navy cushions with ones of rich gold and rust. The comfort I found in my rocking chair with my grandgirls, however, has not gone away. The rhythmic motion of rocking continues to soothe my soul.

My days begin in that rocker. A morning ritual includes drinking green tea and a smoothie made of greens and fruits. As I sit, sipping my elixirs, I check my electronic devices. The gamut runs from perusing social media and checking any unread messages to catching up on current events.

Yesterday can only be described as an awful, interminable one. It actually felt like "The Day Without End." My head gyrated with worry. Superfluous thoughts and trivial details over which I have no control filled my mind to overflowing. I headed out the door for a walk. Walking in the fresh air often provides a source of mental and spiritual renewal for me, the result of introspection and time alone with my Heavenly Father.

That did not happen. As I walked, I felt a sensation on the right side of my knee. Immediately I stepped into that place in my mind where nothing good happens. *I don't want surgery. How am I going to be able to work if I can't walk?* And so the mental merry-go-round took over. My mind escalated into a full-blown, worst-case scenario. Peace was not my friend. I slowed my pace, exercising caution as I walked along oh-so-carefully. I knew beyond a shadow of a doubt an appointment with a surgeon awaited me around the next turn.

Arriving home after a most uninspiring walk, I spent the rest of the afternoon and evening trying to not think about that specific body part in the middle of my leg — the one that bends but also helps hold me upright. You know how well *that* flies, don't you? Instead, thoughts about the knee filled my mind. Finding the focus I needed to deal with the situation before God remained elusive, out of reach.

I thought watching television would be a distraction, but the status of "the knee" took over. *Did it hurt? Did I feel any pain when I moved it? What was that twinge?* The news of the current political climate in our country only exacerbated my sense of helplessness and fear. Oh, the lunacy of us humans.

As I headed for bed, I finally stopped spinning in circles. Then, I could hand over my concerns to God, those affecting my personal life as well as the state of the world. His silence was deafening. *Where are You? I don't see You or hear You. I don't feel You*, was my last thought as I fell asleep.

In the world of meteorology, the weather field, barometers measure pressure in the atmosphere. Weather forecasters observe changes in air pressure that help predict shifts in the weather. If the pressure increases, that often means warmer air and clear skies. Plans can be made for outdoor activities since nice weather is on the way. Decreasing pressure often means cooler air and the formation of clouds due to moisture condensing. Here comes the rain!

I have my own barometer, unrelated to the weather. Connected to my inner being, it indicates accurately whether I am living in the peace provided by my Heavenly Father or in the chaos of the world. My rocking chair fulfills that chore. The speed with which I rock provides the measure.

As I awakened and began my morning ritual, the thought, *I hope this isn't another day like yesterday*, entered my mind. I did not realize the rocking chair had accelerated to such a high rate of speed until I slowed down. When the pace relaxed, I realized I had entered a place of calm.

My knee has improved, though it wasn't the sole contributor to my state of despair and discombobulation the day before. Life as we know it has been tossed up in the air due to a global pandemic and a politically divided country. What will we find when the dust settles? I can attest to the fact that trying to figure that out leads nowhere.

"The Day Without End" did not come to a quiet close. A major storm passed through my area, dumping large amounts of rain. I would have seen the change in air pressure, evidence of its coming, if I had a barometer.

A storm of a different type also passed through my life, creating unrest. The intensity and force of it threatened to upend me. That didn't take place. My rocking chair barometer bore that out—both as the storm came, and as it went.

Peace is my friend. That is, until the next storm passes through. My Heavenly Father continues working with me in love.

> *"Peace I leave with you; my peace I give to you.*
> *I do not give to you as the world gives.*
> *Do not let your hearts be troubled,*
> *and do not let them be afraid."*
> John 14:27

On Giving Thanks in Everything

thanks: n. An expression of gratitude. Grateful feelings or thoughts.

The courtroom stood as a stark statement. Empty. Only those involved in the trial were present: the lawyers, defendant, witnesses, judge, and courtroom officials. Empty. Except for the minister from a small church located in a coastal community and me. No other friends or family members came to support the one on trial.

The defendant, a former neighbor kid, attended church with us before leaving the area. I received his one phone call at the time of his arrest.

The prosecutor presented a mountain of evidence against him, including testimony from the victim of his crime. A guilty verdict seemed inevitable, along with a sentence to serve time. The only remaining questions were where and for how long? Incarceration in the state penitentiary loomed as a very real possibility.

The judge's pronouncement: "Guilty."

In everything give thanks: for this is the will of God passed through my mind. The message did not sound familiar, but I knew it came from God. On returning to my parents' house, where I was staying, I talked with my father about the instructions I'd recalled. Together, we searched and discovered its source in Scripture.

The seed of a new concept planted within me that day. A young man was charged with a crime in a court of law. The judge presiding over that trial deemed him responsible for committing that crime and sentenced him to be incarcerated for two years as punishment. And yet, at the same time, I heard the charge to "give thanks in everything."

By God's grace, the young man avoided the state penitentiary, imprisonment for those who commit major crimes, and went to a correctional institute instead. We stayed in touch during his time there. I wrote letters and sent him a Bible. While in confinement, he determined he would never be incarcerated again. Holding to that conviction and self-promise, he has not.

He and his wife started a long-haul trucking business, taking turns as they drove cross-country. Eventually, they purchased their own truck. He became a successful businessman and an asset to society and his family. His life took a turn, a turn for good, on that fateful day. Though no one saw it at the time, the experience of being held accountable for his actions and behavior turned out to be the crux of a pivotal change for him, a reason to be thankful.

For many, an attitude of thankfulness does not involve a personal being. Instead, it takes the form of abstract, airy-fairy, with the general perception of having "good luck." It doesn't differ much from blowing up a helium balloon, attaching a "Thank You" tag, releasing it, then watching it go up into the sky, where it eventually fades from sight.

I speak of a personal acknowledgement, however, that of giving thanks to God, the giver of all things, "in everything." Therein lies the caveat. Thanking God for all the "feel good" things in life isn't difficult. He asks that I thank Him "in everything." Easy to do? No. It is not.

This much I know: All things are at God's hand. He has a point and purpose in everything. In that I can give thanks.

A young man, having been found guilty of a crime and sentenced to serve time in a correctional facility, provides evidence of the outcome and result of that directive.

Give thanks in all circumstances,
for this is the will of God in Christ Jesus for you.
1 Thessalonians 5:18

On Happiness vs. Joy

happiness: n. The emotion of being happy.

joy: n. A feeling of extreme happiness or cheerfulness, especially related to the acquisition or expectation of something good.

Washing my truck can only be classed as a rare occurrence. I wholeheartedly avoid some tasks in life. Washing a vehicle falls in that category. In my opinion, no other type of dirt compares to road dirt. It is *so* dirty. And gritty and grimy.

The recent fires in my home state of Oregon left a residue of smoke and ash on everything, including my pickup. After my son-in-law told me the sooty film could ruin the paint job, I knew I needed to address the issue. I felt compelled to buy the truck two years ago the minute I spied its sparkly blue finish. God forbid *that* kind of damage should happen.

Arriving home from work, I parked in the driveway instead of entering the garage, an incentive to follow through on the washing project.

The day felt like a "good" one. Only a week earlier, oppressive smoke from the forest fires covered the area I live in, creating the worst air quality of any place on the face of the planet. Local citizens didn't dare even think of going outside. Then the rains came. They dumped water on our dry, thirsty soil, flushing ash-covered surfaces clean.

The truck still needed a good, old-fashioned scrub,

though, and I geared up to tackle the task. Grabbing an old rag, I began the process by filling a bucket with hot water and some Dawn detergent, the recommended cleaner for dealing with ash on vehicles. I had disposable gloves on, but I could feel the warmth of the hot water as I began washing the surface. I started on the passenger side of the truck, making certain I removed all the smoke residue.

Fall had arrived. The shifting of seasons filled the air. My flower beds, including those of my wildflowers, revealed renewal as the gift of rain freshened them.

The wildflower bed in particular brought me great joy. In late spring, while digging through my utility room cupboard, I discovered a package of seeds. The label described it as a Hummingbird and Butterfly Garden Mixture, a combination of reseeding annuals and perennials. The package specified the date for use as four years earlier, so I knew the seeds might not be viable.

Having a wildflower garden has been on my wish list for quite some time, though, so I decided to give it a try. I chose to plant in rock-hard soil with no semblance of anything fertile, but reason had no voice. I dug up a space bordering the sidewalk approximately four feet by twelve feet then added compost from my compost bin and several bags of potting soil. I felt I had nothing to lose.

I sprinkled the seed mix on the area, raked a layer of dirt atop them, and watered it. And watered. And watered some more. The optimum time for planting was so long past, I harbored zero expectations for success. I checked the area often, sometimes several times a day. A magnifying glass would have been helpful in my search for any signs of life.

Imagine my delight when, bit by bit, tiny green leaves peeked up through the surface. Granted, some of them were a nasty, invasive grass weed and volunteer vegetable starts from my compost, which I had to pull out, but other plants sprouted as well.

I continued watering them faithfully, ensuring their roots never dried out. They rewarded me with growth and blossoms. I recognized some of the plants — orange California poppies; pink, blue, and purple bachelor buttons; fragrant garden dill; bright yellow coreopsis and blanket flower; black-eyed Susan; bright pink godetia; red larkspur — and others I have yet to identify. The colors resembled a crazy quilt, a mishmash of blooms and textures. I delighted in their survival and beauty along with the prospect of a perennial garden that will attract bees, butterflies, and hummingbirds.

I had almost completed washing one side of the truck, when I happened to glance up and see a young woman walking down the sidewalk, pushing a baby stroller and chatting with her little girl, the big sister. They stopped by the bed of flowers, the tiny sprite of a girl squatting down to get a closer look. The washing project came to a halt as I became the proverbial "fly on the wall," observing from a distance. I could almost hear their conversation: "Look, Mama — isn't that pink one pretty? Oh, I love the orange one! Will you take a picture of it for me?" Leaning down by her young daughter, the mother pulled out her phone to take photos. After several minutes, they went on their way.

My being filled with pure joy as I watched the young mother and her child admiring God's handiwork.

What, exactly, is joy? Does joy differ from happiness, and in what way?

I have given it a great deal of thought and have no profound revelation or sound explanation, certainly not a spiritual one. From experience, I agree with the dictionary definition: Happiness is emotion; joy is a feeling. I can best describe happiness as taking place in the upper part of my body. The feeling of joy goes the opposite direction, sinking and settling deep within. The blessing and gift of each "joy" experience comes from God. The feeling associated with them cannot be fabricated. Counterfeit efforts, the fake ones, will not, cannot endure.

My wildflower garden has brought me great joy. It has also given joy to others.

And this: If I had been washing the driver's side of the truck instead of the passenger's, my back would have been turned on the entire scene, and I would have missed out. My Heavenly Father motivated me to wash my truck for a reason. As I always say, "It is the little things."

"Happy comes and happy goes, but joy . . . joy plants itself within and reminds us of how good God is." Just me. Just sayin'.

On a God Joy

God Joy: n. A personal experience planned and initiated by our Creator. While you might be an observer, or you might be a participant, it brings a joy that fills to overflowing, and you feel compelled to pass that joy on to others — the joy of God, His love and care. (author's definition)

Even before I got on my hands and knees to scrounge under the bed, I knew I would only find rolls of Christmas wrapping paper stored there. I looked anyway. A search in the hall closet revealed any available gift bags were either Christmas or feminine in nature. I settled on some plain white tissue paper and found some brown ribbon to hold the two packages together. I wanted the gifts to be "just right," but banked on the fact the little boy receiving them probably wouldn't even notice. Or care.

For the past two or three years, I've observed an older gentleman, a neighbor who lives on the other side of the street, waiting for a school bus. In the morning a little guy stands beside him. In the afternoon, he waits alone for the boy's return. I had no personal knowledge or information but assumed he was a grandfather raising a grandson.

In a neighborhood with no other children his age nearby, and school out of session for summer break, the little boy had no playmates. The thought entered unannounced and very quietly: *What could I gift him that would make his time alone more fun?* As the idea settled in, I became more and more excited. I genuinely enjoy being part of a surprise, and I could feel the potential for this one.

It had been a while since I'd been around little boys. What was the current trend? What did he even like? What interested him? I wanted to give something that both suited him and would bring enjoyment.

LEGOS! LEGOS are brightly colored plastic interlocking building blocks that can be used to create whatever one can imagine. I would almost bet money the little boy would like LEGOS.

I did an online shopping search and came up with two items I thought he would enjoy: a spaceship and a dinosaur. Three separate creations could be made using the available LEGOS in each box—six possible from the two. I placed the order and waited for their delivery. Upon arrival, I immediately wrapped them so I could gift them.

Packages in hand, I went to the front door and knocked. I already knew what I was going to say: "My name is Ladonna. I live right across the street from you. I've noticed you have a little boy as your roommate. I have something for him."

The grandfather opened the door, and I delivered the message. The little guy waited inside, out of sight. Grandpa motioned for him to come forward. He introduced me as "the neighbor who lives across the street."

"Are *you* my neighbor?" he asked.

"Yes. This is for you."

His dark-brown eyes went huge behind his glasses. "Is it for my birthday?"

"No. This is a 'just because.' When is your birthday?"

"Friday!" Two days off! What were the odds?

"How old are you going to be?'

"I'm going to be eight."

"Well, this is an early birthday present then."

His grandfather instructed him to thank me, which he did. I told him he might want to open the gifts before thanking me, as he might not like them.

I nailed it on the wrap job. The outer wrapping didn't matter as he excitedly tore it off. The first box he opened contained the LEGOS to build spaceships. "LEGOS! I *love* LEGOS!" The next revealed the one to create dinosaurs. Clutching it to his heart he proclaimed, "I *love* dinosaurs!" My heart filled to overflowing.

As the scene unfolded, the grandfather shared he had been raising Jarron since he was one year old. "I never expected I would be seventy and raising an eight-year-old, but here I am."

"Thank God, he has you. God bless you," was my response.

"It's better than foster care." In a sacrifice of self, this loving grandfather could not allow his grandson to be turned over to the system. And he didn't.

With a broad smile spread across his face, Jarron eagerly stated that "maybe" I could come to his birthday party at his aunt's house. He had already readily welcomed me into his circle.

My visit lasted just a few minutes, but as I turned to leave, his grandpa asked the young boy if he wanted to give me a hug. Oh. My. Heart. This little, almost-eight-years-old boy hugged me and squeezed me with all his might. I melted.

Heading back across the street to my home, my heart burst with joy. And that is the God Joy I want to share with you. May you be as touched by the perfectly planned, coordinated, and timed act of God as I.

I feel personal God experiences are exactly that—personal, not to be publicly broadcast. I am learning, however, that I need to share some so others may see His nature and love, evidenced in "the little things." My encounter with a little boy was nothing about me. It *was* all about Him.

May you, too, hear and listen to that still, small voice within. May you experience God Joys in your life and then share the wealth of His blessings with others.

Finding Solace at My Piano

solace: n. Comfort or consolation in a time of loneliness or distress. A source of comfort or consolation.

The piano with its bench has been a fixture nearly my entire life, both literally and figuratively. The keyboard instrument held court in my parents' living room from the time it left the music store until I had my own home with the necessary accommodation for it.

"Place the piano on an inside wall," the business owner advised them. I have followed suit. Inside walls do not undergo temperature changes in the same way as an outside wall, an important factor in protecting the piano's strings.

The bench cushion has lost its "cush." Its edges and corners reveal batting, which once served as padding. The original threadbare fabric covering obviously had served out its purpose years ago. Yet even though my piano bench is undeniably outdated and scruffy, I would never consider reupholstering it. Whenever I sit down to play, the worn material reminds me of the countless hours I planted my "tush" there. The ancient piece of furniture represents an important part of my life story.

The piano, a small upright spinet—and the bench that came with it—entered my life more than seventy years ago. As a little five-year-old girl, I begged my parents repeatedly to let me take piano lessons. We didn't have a piano, and, though I suspect I listened to one at church services, I don't remember hearing or seeing one played.

My parents typified a generation that went through the Depression—simple, hardworking country folk who spent their money cautiously and shunned waste and lavish spending. I'm quite certain they knew the whims of a small child shift and change with the wind. Investing in a piano and providing money for lessons meant a major outlay of funds. The decision wasn't a casual one. In addition, they did not typically give in to a child's begging and pleading. But they did this time . . . with one condition: "You'll have to practice. Every day."

"Yes." I understood. At the ripe old age of five, I knew the meaning of commitment. The unspoken fact: I could not begin and then change my mind when I decided piano lessons and practicing weren't all that much fun.

The desire came from a passion and drive deep within. I promised to fulfill any and all requirements asked of me. *I wanted to learn how to play.*

As I look back, my mother and father must have made the decision in a step of faith on their part. Five-year-old children don't possess a reputation for having will and resolve.

Mrs. Jacobs, my piano teacher, while being skilled and knowledgeable in her profession, also exuded perfectionism. She presented the picture of a classic lady as she sat erect in her chair at the end of the piano bench with pencil in hand. She used the pencil to make notations on the music or the steno pad where she wrote my practice assignments for the following week. That same pencil became a tool more than once to tap a high wrist or fingers that splayed instead of curved. My music books—Bach, Chopin, Mozart—still bear her written mark, and, as I play, I am conscious of the important role she held in my life. Under her tutelage, I learned discipline, the reward of success, and the joy of making beautiful music.

I took piano lessons for more than twelve years, sometimes practicing three hours a day when preparing for a competition. My mother, who usually stayed in the kitchen or at her sewing machine while I practiced, said she always knew my mood by the way I played. As a kid I didn't notice, but now I realize that, even then, the piano provided a means of expression for me. Dad assessed that I played "with feeling."

I walked away from the piano in my thirties when life became overwhelmed with depression and life lessons. The ability to play with the skill, precision, and technique of my youth had faded. The fingers simply didn't work. As the church pianist, hearing people tell me, "I love listening to you play," served as a wearisome burden when it brought me no joy. I could not continue giving of myself when nothing remained *to* give. For more than thirty years my piano sat as another piece of furniture in the living room, dusted but never used.

Then, out of nowhere, my son asked me to play three songs he had chosen as a present for his fiftieth birthday. All three were difficult—an etude by Chopin, "The Flight of the Bumblebee," and "Malaguena." Decades had passed since I spent any time at the piano, and I knew every possibility existed that I would not be able to master the music . . . even in the most elementary manner. I did a great deal of soul-searching, however, and made the decision to go back to my piano and its bench.

They say, "If you don't use it, you lose it." You may not lose it all, but it does get buried. My niece, a pianist as well, gave me the profound, sage advice to "just show up." And that I did. After nine months of intense, grueling work, I presented him and the rest of my family with a personal concert, in time for his birthday. I did not anticipate that the gift I gave would be given back to me. My piano once again became part of my life.

I call a day like today one of "those" days, the kind I haven't had in years. Typically, I am a morning person, up at the crack of dawn and raring to go. Not today. Today I wanted to crawl back into bed and stay there.

The atmosphere in my country feels like a ton of bricks as division permeates the nation. News reports commonly discuss a racial divide among its citizens. Political differences bear the classification of either "right" or left," with no consideration given to finding common ground.

Voicing one's thoughts or opinions may be challenged as being false, besides being condemned by those who disagree. Hatred is palpable and toxic. Many have no regard for law as destruction runs unbridled. Right has become wrong; truth is called lie. The unknown and uncertain future awaits with a cloud of grave concern.

My piano beckoned. I sat down on the familiar, timeworn bench and began to play. How do I express what it feels like to pour out your feelings through your fingers? No words can satisfactorily describe the two-fold experience, where the performer also becomes the audience.

As my fingers moved across the keys, something

happened. I became aware of my Heavenly Father listening. The music flowed from my fingertips then came back to my ears and entered my being. My eyes filled with tears, the sanctity of the moment touching me.

When I finished, I stood up and pushed the relic of a bench back in its place under the piano. Peace had settled in my spirit.

The need to be comforted and the means of finding comfort or solace is individual and personal. For some, it may be discovered in a long walk. Others may be given comfort while curling up in a blanket in front of a fireplace with a book and a cup of tea. Another might obtain solace watching a thunder and lightning storm from inside the safety of their home. The possibilities have no limits. On a personal level, today I found solace at my piano while in the presence of God.

Wherever you are, whatever is going on in your life, may you find solace as well.

> *"Blessed are those that mourn,*
> *for they will be comforted."*
> Matthew 5:4

On Gathering Together with Charlie

"Charlie. Charlie Owens," he said, attaching a name to the twinkling, dark-brown eyes and flash of a grin. I had gone to the local mail center to purchase stamps so I could mail the July invoices for my gardening business, a long overdue task. Since it was well into September, I had no excuses. He had come in to have copies made on the copy machine, "three of them."

Walking cautiously with a cane as he placed his feet with care, I could see at a casual glance that he lives with, and knows, pain. His stature indicated God declared him perfect when He completed his physical creation at a little over five feet in height.

The summer of 2017 brought unprecedented devastation to my home state of Oregon in the form of wind-fueled fire, ravaging its lush green growth and forestland. Blackened tree trunks and devastating desolation replaced its natural beauty, leaving a bare moonscape in many areas. It is not an exaggeration to say the state blazed, with no end in sight. Lack of rain and very hot weather conditions intensified any efforts to bring the forest fires under control.

A grim smoke cover dominated, blocking out the blue skies of glorious, sunny summer days. The sun and moon took on a red hue. Hazardous breathing conditions became prevalent because of the pollution in the air. The advisory issued to the citizenry instructed them to "Stay indoors" and "wear a breathing mask if going outside." Refuge and escape from the blight of fire did not exist.

I completed affixing stamps to envelopes and the gentleman had paid for his copies when the two of us began talking about the long-term damage of the fires to the timber industry. In former days, he worked for a large timber company. We discovered we had a mutual acquaintance, a family member of mine who worked for the same company. It was then he introduced himself, with the request to pass on greetings.

The mail center had no other customers, so we stood and talked for quite a while—of the current ruination affecting our state, of family, and of faith.

Our conversation revealed we shared similar values and personal spiritual beliefs. He talked about being an altar boy, of his marriage to the "perfect" woman, and the values of respect and love taught by his father. We agreed that God needs to be the base of life, from which all else springs. And that people need to "look up" instead of focusing on the catastrophes taking place.

"I'm short," he said with a smile on his face and a chuckle in his voice as he lifted his eyes skyward. "There's no place for me to look but up."

At the age of sixty-nine, he and his wife have eighteen children, two of them still at home. The family prays together twice a day, as the day begins and as the day ends. They encourage any who gather around the table with them to share their daily experiences and any needs or concerns.

Charlie explained that each person matters and all benefit from their contributions. "What a gift of faith you are giving your children," I told him. "Of faith *and* hope."

Heading out the front door, we continued visiting. "You are a delight," I told him. "I am so thankful to have met you. And this, right here, is just one of the reasons I believe."

Charlie nodded in agreement, his bright smile and demeanor touching me. "I know," he said. "I thought I was just coming down to have three copies made, and He had other plans."

"He is the great choreographer," I added.

Many make a strong case for church attendance and membership, citing the Scripture: *"For where two or three are gathered in my name, I am there among them."*[11]

Charlie Owens and I would never have met in a church, never have shared our faith and our lives. A church bulletin did not schedule the encounter, predetermined and organized. And it didn't take place on a Sunday or a Wednesday evening.

Yet there we were, in the middle of a Pak Mail office, the "two gathered together."

---

[11] Matthew 18:20

On Being a Representative

representative: n. Someone who represents others as a member of a legislative or governing body.

represent: v. To stand or act in the place of; to perform the duties, exercise the rights, or otherwise act on behalf of.

The thought was a simple one: *Stop by the local grocery store, purchase a bouquet of flowers, and take them to a friend dealing with a reboot of cancer.* I didn't need to visit. Her body, mind, and soul are spent. I would leave the rays of sunshine at her front door to be discovered long after I had come and gone.

For myself, I know the source of these thoughts and ideas. As a person of faith, my Heavenly Father sends them my way. I can choose to act upon them. Or not.

Mission accomplished. My heart went out to the recipient, her incalculable needs, and the bright joy sent her way from the mind of her Heavenly Father. I searched for the words to thank God for including me, for letting me in on His secret surprise. No adequate words came to mind.

Some in religious circles apply the phrase "being used by God." I stumbled over those words. "Being used" seems to have such a negative connotation, far removed from the character and nature of our Creator. He is anything and everything but . . . a user.

Finally, I had the words to thank Him: *Thank You for choosing me to be part of Your plan.* Very quietly, He reminded me that He whispered years ago: "I have chosen you to represent Me."

When we think about representatives, our mind goes to those in government we have elected to a position of power and authority. Their primary role is to fulfill the will of the people, not of self. However, being a representative can be found in other areas besides the world of politics. Consider the meanderings of my mind.

People everywhere fill that role. You may represent someone or some*thing*. Perhaps it falls into the category of a philosophy, an ideology, a value, a point of character, a cause, or any number of other things.

For example, I may be a proponent of the Second Amendment, with a personal arsenal of guns and ammunition. It would be fair to say I represent that cause. Perhaps I plant my garden with shrubs and flowers that are native to my particular area. It could be said I represent an earth-first philosophy. Do you advocate hard work and accountability? Without a doubt, your life represents those qualities. The lives of many represent the results of a bad choice or decision. Others might represent a life filled with greed, pride, or decadence. We represent those things that are important to us, evidenced in the way we live our lives.

For those of faith, we who have chosen to live with God, He has, in turn, chosen *us* to represent Him, to be His voice, His hands and feet. May we represent Him well—in our home, with friends and family, at work, in the presence of people we know and those we don't—so that He might be seen in this world. And, remember, as in the world of politics, His representatives are to fulfill the will of the One they represent—not of self.

We are God's representative. You could ask for no higher calling. Nor could I.

> *"Let your light shine before others,*
> *so that they may see your good works*
> *and give glory to your Father in heaven."*
> Matthew 5:16

The Voice That Came Out of Nowhere

Imagine with me, if you will: You're a young teenage boy, walking home after school with your buddy. You pass a row of mailboxes and open one of them. You remove the mail and then you close the lid. *But* . . . as you turn to head homeward, you hear out of nowhere, "Put that back!" You stop dead in your tracks as the two of you try to figure out where the voice came from. Unable to determine its source, you continue walking down the sidewalk, envelope in hand.

"That doesn't belong to you! Put it back!" Somehow, this time that does sound like a good idea, so you backtrack and return the mail to its rightful recipient, in the mailbox. The voice hasn't finished, though. "Don't you have any manners!? Don't you ever do that again! Ever!"

The timing can only be called "perfect, impeccable, precise," or even "divine." A ten-second window existed that allowed me to be privy to the incident. Typically, I do not spend my days looking out the front window. But I had filled my bird feeder earlier in the day and entertained myself by watching the sweet little birds enjoying their feast. I had opened the windows in order to revel in the fresh fall air. Kids from the middle school, a block away, flooded the sidewalk at the end of the school day. Those two boys just happened to enter my line of vision.

In truth, I was more than privy. The voice that came out of nowhere belonged to *me*. The kids heard me clearly, because I yelled loudly through the wide-open window.

I initially reacted to my outlandish response by concluding that I am, perhaps, a crotchety, old woman. The sobering possibility gave me pause.

The outdoors beckoned me. I put on my walking shoes. I needed to quietly reflect on what had taken place. An afternoon walk sounded perfect.

Thoughts and questions filled my mind as I walked. Did God want the young man to learn a lesson from the incident? Did he tell anyone, including his parents, about "the voice that came out of nowhere?" Probably not. He would have to admit his theft. Did it affect him? Did the experience scare him? I have no idea.

I must admit the voice that came out of nowhere surprised me too. I had no idea I could be so aggressive in taking a stand against a wrongful act. What did I need to see about myself?

The walk helped to sort things out. I am not a crotchety, old woman, but I *am* an instrument, a voice for the Most High God. Happenstance does not exist in God's world. Our Creator coordinates all things in life. I said a little prayer for the young man, asking God to use a mailbox and a voice that came out of nowhere in ways only He can. In the meantime, I can't help but wonder if that poor kid is going to have nightmares, thinking a ghost was haunting him.

You just never know what your day is going to bring. I suspect one young man would agree.

Live Life Like a Golfer

golf: n. A ball game played by individuals competing against one another in which the object is to hit a ball into each of a series of (usually nine or eighteen) holes in the minimum number of strokes.

"I feel so overwhelmed if I think of the overall picture. So I'm just going to go with your 'one step at a time.'"

A friend has set aside her nurse's cap to train for another job, that of a medical coder. At the age of seventy-two, with a bad knee to boot, her body could no longer hold up to the physical rigors and demands of nursing. A desk job, one that relies on brains *sans* brawn, seemed practical and makes sense. She returned to school at the local community college to gain certification and future employment.

"Why," you may ask, "does she still need to work? Don't nurses make good money?" A bout with cancer several years ago wiped her out financially. Period.

Panic set in as she began her second term. "It's the 2:30 a.m. wake-up thoughts. Last night it was, *What am I doing? What if I fail?* I'm trying to not get that panicky, overwhelming feeling thinking about it."

"You're trying to take on the whole," I had told her. "It will never work. You can only go one day at a time, one step at a time,"

Life is like that. The entirety of it can be overwhelming. It may present itself in the form of family concerns, health issues, financial problems, or, in our present culture, be political in nature. In reality, we only possess right here, right now, this current moment in time. To be concerned about "someday" wastes an enormous amount of time and energy. The efforts can be perfectly described as an exercise in futility.

My suggestion: Live life like a golfer. The game of golf consists of either nine or eighteen holes. The point of the game is quite simple. The golfer strives to hit a small ball, using a golf club, into each of those holes with the least number of swings (called strokes) possible. A player can only complete the course by hitting the ball toward each hole one hit, one swing, at a time. Sometimes the ball goes in water or high grass and can't even be seen or found. Another one takes its place, and the golfer continues, one swing at a time. The final stroke on the final hole completes the game.

When the game begins at the first hole, the final destination isn't even visible. The layout of the course, with a flag indicating the next hole, creates a natural path toward the last hole, marking the end of the game.

This is my point: Deal with the task at hand in the here and now. The process cannot be sped up. Take every step in order, and you will eventually reach the end.

Regardless of your personal circumstances, the picture is clear and makes sense.

So go forth. Live life like a golfer. Focus on the here and now, those things right in front of you. Take one step, one day at a time. But never forget the final goal, even though you can't see it. For me, that means finishing out this physical life and stepping into eternity.

*"Do not worry about tomorrow,
for tomorrow will bring worries of its own."*
Matthew 6:34

III
Food for Thought

Food for thought: n. Something that should be thought about or considered carefully.

On Being Human

human: n. A person.[12]

I could only describe this past week as "one of *those* weeks." Some *are* harder than others. I found myself feeling at every turn that I either said or did something stupid, intrusive, or out of order. "Open mouth. Insert foot" could easily qualify as my theme song.

Why can't I keep my mouth shut? Why did I do that? What was I thinking? Right — I wasn't thinking!

This sort of behavior shoots me off, continually second-guessing myself. Instead of readily flowing, I become hesitant then apologize for things I have said or done. God has not taught me to live this way, but nonetheless that's where I've been — in a state where I heard myself say as I awakened in the morning, "I'm so tired of being human."

When I first began my spiritual walk, in innocence and naivete, I had an unrealistic picture of life. I felt I was something special, a bit (a lot!) better than others. My pious "spiritual" attitude became my virtual sidekick, my humanity clothed in self-righteousness. When anger, doubt, impatience, or fear manifested itself in the reality of living everyday life, I readily propelled into a tailspin of self-condemnation.

---

[12] *The American Heritage Dictionary of the English Language,* 5th Edition, https://ahdictionary.com/word/search.html?q=Human, accessed February 15, 2025.

One particular time, I shared a "failure" with a friend. I hadn't lived up to my expectations of what I thought I should be like or how I should be living. Her response: "What are you expecting? You are human."

Boy! Am I ever!

Even though I have a lifetime of experience with my loving, kind Heavenly Father, I struggle with finding peace. I wrestle with doubt. I question myself. I criticize aspects of my interaction with others.

Life brings with it adversities and challenges. There may be a health issue with a parent, a child struggling to find their way. The bottom might drop out of personal budgets as a costly automobile or home repair comes out of nowhere. Family dynamics may become toxic with no ready resolution available. Patience comes easily when stress or pressure doesn't prevail. Being kind and caring is a piece of cake when all is well with, and in, the world. Difficult circumstances reveal the truth of our character *and* our faith.

My walk with God began decades ago. He has continually pushed me beyond my limits, shored me up, and ministered to me. As a *bona fide* old lady, I can attest to His presence in every aspect of life.

I am human, with more than enough flaws, warts, and foibles to confirm that. This fact also places me on the same plane as every other person in this world. I am no better. I am no worse. If anything of any value manifests in my life, it is the result of His work—not mine.

I am human and in good company, that of the person of Christ. He laid aside His cape of glory, replacing it with the rags of humanity. While He never succumbed to "The Three

S's of Satan, Sin, and Self," He knew and understood the human factor and now intercedes on my behalf before God. While walking this earth, I wonder if He ever awakened with the same thought: *I'm so tired of being human.*

God knows my heart. He loves and accepts me in my present state. Self-acceptance, including my humanness, is necessary and important.

God's universal message of love, repentance, and renewal resounds with the truth and hope that He neither judges nor condemns us for being human. We do that to ourselves.

> *And the Word became flesh and lived among us.*
> John 1:14

On a Pair of Walking Shoes

empathy: n. Identification with or understanding of the thoughts, feelings, or emotional state of another person.

My shoes grabbed my attention as I started walking down the sidewalk. I hadn't gone very far, but I found them quite intriguing, with their own story to tell.

I've made it a goal to walk with regularity since I retired from my gardening business—even if only for a short distance. The brief physical activity doesn't begin to replace the number of steps I tallied per day behind a mower. However, my body and mind feel better when I'm moving in the fresh air. *I* feel better.

My daughter gifted me the shoes before we left for Scotland and Ireland three years earlier. She knew our trip would involve a lot of walking. Even though I didn't try them on before purchase, they fit perfectly.

While well-worn, they still remain serviceable. Their soles reveal my personal gait. The tread on the outside heel of each shoe shows a great deal of wear, an indication of the way I roll my foot from the outside to the inside with each step. This always proved to be a source of great consternation for my poor mother while I was growing up. "You're so hard on shoes! Your brothers don't need new shoes nearly as often as you do." The obvious message—I needed to walk differently. I never did. I still don't.

The shoes triggered a flood of memories. I remember wearing them while standing on the shores of Loch Lomond in Scotland with my daughter and my grandgirl. I wore them when I climbed the Cliffs of Moher in Ireland, a vertical equivalent of eight flights of stairs. They went to Edinburgh Castle and wandered through Windsor Castle in London. These shoes have covered miles and miles of pavement.

And here I am, wearing them while walking on a sidewalk in Eugene, Oregon.

No one would ever know the journeys my shoes have taken by looking at them. No one would know where *I* have been by looking at me.

My thoughts led to an obvious point, the crux. Every pair of shoes tells a story. That story belongs to the one wearing them. No two stories are alike, because no two people are alike.

Usually, when we look at another person, we see only physical characteristics or personal attributes. The next time you see someone and, perhaps, find you're ready to criticize or judge, look at their shoes. Don't focus on the style, color, or design, but consider *their* story and that of the person wearing them.

We cannot know the state of another, be it mental, physical, spiritual, or financial. No one can know where a person has been, their history, or their present circumstances. Try to withhold judgment. A little bit of compassion, empathy, and kindness goes a long way in how we treat people. A lot goes even further.

"You can't understand someone until you've walked a mile in their shoes."
Unknown

A Majority of One

majority: More than half (50 percent) of some group. The difference between the winning vote and the rest of the votes.

minority: Any subgroup that does not form a numerical majority.

The little ragamuffin of a girl, all of eight or nine years old, stood facing the opposition of the world, at least the world as she knew it. She and a classmate had a disagreement during recess on the playground at the small country grade school she attended. In a stand-off between the two, fellow students joined in support of her opponent.

While the situation did not have the importance of a David and Goliath moment, no one stood on the side of the little girl as hostility spewed from the mouths of those who became judge and jury. In frustration, she picked up a fir cone from the ground and threw it at her adversary. Widely missing its mark, the action prompted ridicule and more heated comments. Mercy intervened when the bell rang, signaling the end of recess and time to return to the classroom.

Even the most casual of observers would have noted I, as the little girl, was in the minority, not the majority.

Recently, a client and I had a conversation about those in our country who belong to a racial minority. She expressed some of the inequities they face, the injustices meted out based solely on skin color. We concurred that, as Caucasians, neither of us has had similar experiences of prejudice.

I heard myself say, "*I* am part of a minority." I certainly did not intend *those* words to come out of my mouth. In the two decades as the owner/operator of my gardening business, I made it a policy to refrain from discussing controversial subjects, such as politics or religion, with my clients. But there it was. The incredulous expression on her face translated into speechlessness as she tried to comprehend what she had just heard.

I weighed my words carefully, wanting to make certain she understood, without provoking ire. "I am a person of faith. We are a minority in this country." I went on to explain that one who practices the tenets of a certain religion or attends church does not fall into the same category. I expressed that a person of faith has a relationship with God, our Creator. I told her one need only look at the policies of our country, where a concerted effort has taken place to remove God or any mention of Him from our culture. She could not deny that truth and didn't try.

Majorities and minorities boil down to the numbers, and they translate into power. The more numbers, the more power. Simple, but true.

The little ragamuffin girl remains a part of my makeup and who I am. I have always wanted to be on the winning side. I suspect that it does not make me unique. Most people don't like losing.

Recent events of lawlessness, immorality, and corruption would suggest that I *am* on the losing side. The majority in my country do not celebrate my principles and beliefs as a person of faith.

We can live life one of two ways: following God as a person of faith or following self-interests. Two very distinctive, different paths exist. One, a wide road, jam-packed with people, that leads to death. The other, a solitary one that leads to life. My way of life and its narrow path does not win any popularity contests.

If I look at the numbers, the evidence strongly points to the reality that I belong to the minority in these times. But the numbers do not tell the whole story.

I'm not on the losing side. I stand with God. He stands with me. *He* is a majority of one.

What then are we to say about these things?
If God is for us, who is against us?
Romans 8:31

On Thinking for Yourself

think: v. To ponder, to go over in one's head.

I spend quite a bit of time thinking. Allow me to extol the virtues of thinking. As one raised in an environment where those around me did not particularly promote self-thought, I know the difference. No one told me what to think. However, I sensed the parameters of any given subject and knew the acceptable position surrounding them. Over time, I adopted those thoughts as my own and enjoyed the approval that resulted. I fit in.

I maintain humankind does this all the time, young or old, in all varieties of circles — religious, academic, political, social, and familial. Life sometimes feels easier when someone either tells you what to think or you simply accept the current narrative. Besides, thought that differs from the norm may be viewed as controversial, so people make a point of skirting the subject.

At first, thinking for myself proved to be very difficult. All kinds of thoughts ricocheted around in my mind before I settled down to conscious assessment. Even now, I often approach a situation or a problem with the question, "What *do* I think?"

Thinking differs from worry. Worry is negative and nonproductive. Talk about going in circles! Worry will do that every time. God created us with the ability for thought, so thinking is elemental. Thinking provides the basis of decision-making, opinion, belief, and conviction, or an action. It may mean a simple assessment of facts, or might include one's emotions, history, and experiences. Giving thought to a situation or problem is productive, often culminating in a conclusion.

No one else in the world thinks as I do. My thoughts emanate from within my mind and belong to me alone . . . as do yours. Thoughts fall into the category of being as individual and as unique as DNA and fingerprints. All thoughts are personal and private. Others become privy to them only if we share them.

Our Creator has gifted each person the capacity for thought. Don't squander it or turn control of it over to another. Use it wisely.

On Being Real

real: adj. Genuine, not artificial, counterfeit, or fake.

My son worked for a pizza company that extolled its use of real cheese as a major advertising point. Who even knew fake cheese existed? That enigma became one of my first exposures to the world of "artificialdom," a world that has escalated to the present, one where "things are not as they seem to be." Much of what we see and experience is not real.

Several years ago, I went into a recording studio and made a CD of several piano renditions. While *I* performed at the piano, the finished product could not be called real. I did not play the music as mistake-free as it sounded.

The recording world calls the process editing. The producer has the capability of electronically maneuvering notes, altering the tempo, and manipulating the volume as well. The gentleman recording my music told me repeatedly, "This is how CDs are made."

In our daily lives, we view manipulated photographs, listen to electronically contrived music, and hear distorted accounts of current events. AI, Artificial Intelligence, bombards our world. Not all that long ago, many of us had no awareness or even a rudimentary understanding of AI, let alone the role it plays in everyday life. We are only now beginning to comprehend the vast scope of artificial self-creation and its effects.

Even though the physical world we live in overflows with everything fake, I hold to the importance of being real as a person. What do I mean by that? I believe each of us began our lives in a state of being real. Over time, that authenticity was compromised. Perhaps a parent required us to say "I'm sorry" to a sibling when we felt anything *but*—sorry, that is. Perhaps a teacher expected "good" behavior so order could be maintained in the classroom. Maybe spouses, friends, or family members asked for concessions to help maintain a semblance of peace. Trying to please people takes its toll. The constant need to self-edit can be overwhelming.

Over time, this results in the compromise of self—how we feel and what we think. From my personal experience, *I* became so neutralized I didn't even know myself. As I said, trying to please people does take its toll.

The façades and layers of phony images that build up over a lifetime take time to be exposed and dealt with. Similar to an onion, layer after layer must be peeled back in order to uncover the real person. For me personally, exposure happened as I spent time in the presence of God. Discovery took place as I became acquainted with the person I really am, the one God created. I found the process unnerving at times because I didn't know who or what I was going to find. Or if I would even like *what* I found.

The big reveal turned out to be the child within me. I never stopped being a five-year-old at heart—the stubborn, outspoken one who loved life and laughter, talked a lot, and drove her parents up the wall with her "busyness." The expectations and requirements had simply buried her.

I like the person I found. I am real. For me, the result made the sometimes-difficult process worth it. I highly recommend the state and place of being real. Try it. You will like it.

On Weeds in Your Garden

weeds: (plural) Any plant unwanted at the place . . . and time it is growing.

I planned to get out in my garden early, before the day heated up. I neglected to factor in one aspect, though. I wanted to weed the bed on the south side of the house—the sunniest area in the garden. I would need to be out there before sunrise or after sunset in order to avoid the direct sunlight. Undeterred and resolved to get the bed cleaned up, I plopped on a sun hat, grabbed the garden tools, and headed forth on my mission.

Weeds in the garden are a constant battle. I'm on my third round this season, trying to bring them under control. I think I've finished, turn around, and find them smiling brightly at me. And so I begin again.

One particular weed has plagued me ever since I brought home some cheap bird seed that had an abundance of filler seeds. The birds happily spread them throughout my garden space. In addition to flourishing in nurtured soil, the aggressive rogue grass has no problem taking up residence in the sidewalk cracks and flooding the rock pathway. Only God knows how many seeds and potential plants exist in a single seedhead. And each plant has plenty of them. If I miss one weed, it goes to seed, and the dirty deed repeats itself.

I'm very methodical when I deal with a task like this. I

begin at one end of the garden bed and plod along, never looking up to see how far I've come or how much more remains. In the meantime, my mind might be blank, void of any thoughts. Sometimes, recent events and details of my life may circulate through, stirring up brain activity. Other times, I go into "deep thought." Today was one of *those* days.

Some people with a right-to-live philosophy feel weeds are virtuous and need to be treated with respect so they can co-exist in a garden. I do not deny or negate their fact of creation by an intelligent God, but I also consider their nature and growth habit. In my garden, co-existence is unacceptable. A weed left untended, such as that rascally grass, will dominate, denying all other plants nourishment and water. A non-weed plant cannot compete, as its roots become constricted and its growing area overcome. Therefore, in a garden of either beauty or vegetables, weeds cannot be ignored. They must be dealt with. And, for me, that means removal.

When it comes to getting rid of weeds, a half-hearted or half-measure approach will fail. They must be removed completely, by the roots. If any hair roots remain in the soil, they sprout again. Most domestic garden plants, whose sole purpose consists of either blooming or wearing beautiful foliage, will die if you damage their roots or stalk. Whereas a weed will reappear and shout, "Hello! You thought you got rid of me, didn't you?"

Where *do* weeds come from? They come from seeds. What is the viability life of a seed? The record belongs to a 2,000-year-old date palm seed, which is the oldest ever germinated. Six-hundred-year-old mustard seeds germinated after being excavated from a Denmark monastery.

Most weed seeds in a typical garden won't last that long, but some, such as Canada thistle, can last up to two decades.[13] I've read that many weed seeds lie dormant in the soil for up to ten years. When we cultivate the soil, we actually bring those seeds to the surface, where they respond to sun and water. It's ironic, isn't it? While attempting to rid our garden of weeds, we actually create a favorable environment for them to thrive.

Even if a person doesn't have a physical garden, and no desire to tend one, we humans have an inner garden, a spiritual one. Tending this garden is extremely important and affects our ability to live well. Or not.

What constitutes a spiritual weed? And how can it be removed so our inner garden thrives? I would say anything that distracts, restricts, or prohibits us from living a righteous life can easily be labeled a spiritual weed. If a habit or character issue prevents us from a life of fulfillment, one with peace and joy, *then* we have a weed problem. And the Master Gardener needs to do some weed removal, getting to the root of the issue.

Perhaps now would be a good time to sit and take a good, long, hard look in the proverbial mirror. What in your life always gets in the way of relationships and health, preventing living life to the fullest? Maybe it's a life-long habit. There might be a personal trait about yourself you've tried to change unsuccessfully, such as selfishness or anger. Then again, perhaps it's something like regret or bitterness that consistently and persistently hinders your freedom to live unencumbered.

---

[13] Laura Miller, "These Weeds That Spread By Seed Can Sprout After Years," published April 15, 2023, Gardeningknowhow.com

You may or may not believe in God. The truth is you have been created by Him. He loves you and cares about every detail of your life. Take an honest, personal assessment of yourself before Him. After all, most of us want to live the best version of ourselves, don't we?

That can only happen at His Hand. As *the* Master Gardener, He possesses the capability to get those spiritual weeds out by the root.

I finished weeding the bed. I even accomplished more than I expected when I grubbed the evil grass weed from the rock pathway. Am I finished? Of course not. More areas needing weed removal abound, both in my physical garden and my spiritual garden.

As much as I despise them, the weeds in my garden never magically disappear during the night while I sleep. I have to deal with them in a personal manner. That same truth applies to spiritual weeds. I need to plant myself before God so He can shed light on my inner garden and remove the weeds.

I challenge you to do the same. It *is* the only way to become the best version of *you*!

On Priorities

priority: n. An item's relative importance.

The floor has needed vacuuming for days and days. Plus, the furniture begs to be dusted. I would like to say I clean religiously on a weekly basis, but I don't. I never perfected a routine cleaning system and, at this point in my life, never will. My impulsive nature results in dealing with things when the urge hits. I guess you could say a regular cleaning schedule doesn't rate as a high priority with me.

My days often begin before sunrise. I usually wake up and crawl out of bed by 5:00 or 5:30. The habit began many years ago when I had four children at home. I treasured the very early morning as the one time of day I could call my own. After the children left home, that practice continued. A cup of green tea, spending time at the piano or the computer, working on Christmas ornaments for the family, visiting with friends on the phone. There's nothing like the crack of dawn to accomplish these. If I had to categorize this time in my daily life, I would most certainly place it at the top of the list as a priority.

A priority resembles a yardstick that measures the level of importance something holds in a person's life. The mark will register high, low, or somewhere in between. Each of us has our own most important ones that factor into and even motivate or control our lives. For some, education might fall in a category of high priority. For others, financial worth, a circle of friends, or business contacts matter the most. A priority may also include political or environmental causes, church, health and fitness, and hobbies or sports interests. The broad range varies, as individual and unique as each person.

A window opens deep into a person's being with the revelation of their priorities. Priorities make an undeniable statement without words, explanations, or definition. They honestly represent what a person deems to be of value. We invest our time, our money, and ourselves in those things that are most important to us.

The true worth of a priority, however, becomes exposed when measured against God, life, and eternity. Will it matter in the end? Is it eternal? Perhaps now would be a good time for a reality check.

Personally, my life springs from two base priorities: God and family. I view Him as the Author and Source of my life. My family comes second only after Him.

The urge to vacuum hit. I am hoping I will have that same kind of inclination to mow my lawn. Apparently, the care and upkeep of my yard isn't a high priority either. While I still worked, a friend asked what I would do if I retired. I responded that I would probably have a cleaner house and a yard I enjoy. I can hope, but time will tell. They may not be much of a priority after all.

> *"For where your treasure is,*
> *there your heart will be also."*
> Matthew 6:21

On Choices

choice: n. An option; a decision; an opportunity to choose or select something.

Time spent in my own garden is rare. As a self-employed gardener, my clients' gardens and their needs always take precedence over mine. In the middle of the growing season, the to-do list for them overwhelms me. I put blinders on my eyes when I pull into my driveway so I don't have to look at my garden's unkempt state.

I'm not sure how it happened that I arrived home at a decent hour today, but I did. Plenty of daylight remained, and, after feeding myself, I had the energy to head outdoors. I decided to work in the part of my backyard most visible from inside my house. I wanted to view the fruit of my labor as I looked out the window. Weeds blanketed the area. I began the hands-and-knees kind of work, the kind that frees one's mind for thought.

Earlier in the day I read the comment, "It costs $0 to be decent." As I vigorously addressed the patch of weeds, my mind wandered: *What does it cost to be a jerk?* While I thought about it, I concluded the difference between the two is simple—the result of a choice.

Choice fills everyday life: *What am I going to eat? How do I dress? Where am I going, and what am I going to do? How do I get there and when?* Thoughtful consideration reveals that, in our daily lives, making choices confronts us in a nonstop manner.

In addition, our materialistic society has made it a priority to attempt to satisfy the consumer's desires, young and old alike. When purchasing a car, carpeting, an appliance, or furniture, the list of choices seems endless — color, style, price, quality, on and on. Likewise, when shopping for clothing, planning a meal out, or even a vacation. Humankind's narcissistic appetite for self-satisfaction and self-indulgence seems to be driving this state, and the moneymakers of the world readily comply.

A prevalent trend in child-rearing has surfaced as many parents abdicate their responsibilities of decision-making. "What do *you* want to eat (or wear or do)?" they ask their children, off-loading the burden of choice and its consequences onto the child. I cannot adamantly call this unilaterally negative. The approach certainly contrasts with the "children should be seen and not heard" philosophy of days gone by. Children *should* be treated as people, allowed to give input and express their opinions. I feel, however, parents need to fill *their* role of guiding their charges in the process of making decisions and choices instead of transferring that job onto their children. A kid shouldn't be asked to perform the overwhelming task of coping as an adult.

The more important choices I reference, however, have to do with the ones made as to how one lives their life, not just the decisions affecting the physical, outer aspect of it.

As I dug through the weeds, I found myself thinking about how, beginning at an early age, we choose the kind of people we want to be. Sometimes we make a conscious decision, other times unconscious. A personal experience or incident in our lives may play a role, though we might never describe it as a choice.

When I was a young girl, my older brother brought a typewriter into our home to work on a school project. I vividly remember it sitting on the card table in the middle of the living room. "Don't touch it!" The instructions given to me could not have been more specific.

I had never seen a typewriter up close and personal before. I wrestled with the temptation . . . and the instructions. I couldn't resist messing with it. Apparently, I didn't cover my tracks very well. The disobedience must have been obvious. When questioned, I denied my actions. The lie felt worse than the disobedience. The seed of truth and honesty planted itself within me and began to grow.

One young woman I know lives by the mantra, "Do to others as you would have them do to you."[14] She has made that Scripture the foundation of how she lives her life and what she teaches her children. As a child, she experienced harsh treatment, not only from peers but from an adult teacher as well. She made a choice to live differently.

I decide whether or not I will be kind or unkind, forgiving instead of bitter, spiteful, or vindictive. I can opt to be loving and compassionate instead of hateful and distant. I make the choice to be cooperative, not antagonistic; humble rather than proud and boastful. No other person decides if I will be generous, selfless, and charitable in contrast to self-serving; decent rather than a jerk. The way I live my life, the kind of person I choose to be sits in my lap and is reflected in my mirror. That never falls on another person's doorstep.

---

[14] Matthew 7:12 NIV

Our Creator has given humans free will and free choice. Use it carefully and wisely, not only in determining allegiance to Him — or not — but in living life. Choices matter.

*"If you are not willing to serve him,
decide today whom you will serve,
the gods your ancestors worshiped in Mesopotamia
or the gods of the Amorites . . .
As for my family and me, we will serve the* LORD.*"*
Joshua 24:15 GNT

On Contrast and Comparison

contrast: n. Something that is opposite of or strikingly different from something else.

comparison: n. An evaluation of the similarities and differences of one or more things relative to some other or each other.

Hot or cold. Day or night. Light or dark. Rich or poor. Sickness or health.

Contrasts and comparisons comprise a good part of everyday life. We often make such assessments without conscious thought or even awareness of doing so. We compare the temperature one day to the next, service at the local restaurant, shampoos, our rest from one night to another, *ad infinitum.*

My appetite disappeared. The thought of food had no appeal, not even that of bulk food bin #2001, a chocolate/nut mix favorite at the local grocer. I knew then I was physically ill, not just languishing in a mentally laggard state of slothfulness. Sometimes my mind needs to get in gear before my body decides to go to work, and I'd assumed that was the case. The lack of desire for any food verified otherwise.

For several days I had been pushing myself, dragging my heels. The previous day I heard myself say repeatedly, "I don't feel well." The loss of appetite clinched the matter, proof positive the situation was physical not mental. Feeling ill compared to feeling well.

The concept of contrast and comparison can be a valuable tool in life, one that provides perspective and aids in bringing understanding to many experiences in life, often a before-and-after picture.

I lived with, and struggled with, deep depression for many years. Its constant presence and never-ending state felt like a plague and a curse. I never cease to revel in the life I now live and know, a picture of contrast and comparison. I feel I value and appreciate my current state more because of being trapped in the former one.

My heart goes out to those who struggle. I would never have the same capacity for understanding or care for others had I not resided in that place myself. I knew and experienced the hell-hole depths of darkness and hopelessness of life. At the same time, I now carry a sense of hope and possibility for others.

Other areas in my life exist where, as I compare, I see contrast as well. Insights reveal changes in my former inner state vs. the present. I have been given a clear mind, replacing mental chaos and a mind so filled with debris that thought processes were difficult. I can hear and sense my Creator. To think. And to reason. Laughter has replaced tears. What a glorious gift! I no longer live under the bondage of obsessive, addictive behavior but in freedom. Yes, it is possible! A grim outlook of absolute hopelessness and negativism has changed into a bright, positive outlook. A life of lies and darkness switched to living a life in truth and light. What was is no more.

Why do bad things happen to good people? I propose substituting the word "hard" for "bad." Life's experiences may seem hard, but that doesn't make them bad. In fact, they are the opposite, proving to be invaluable in stretching us, developing maturity, and producing compassion, empathy, and understanding for others.

Hard times deepen us. Circumstances designed by God provide the opportunity to become a better, different kind of person, one more fully reflecting His image. Circumstances change us. This, in contrast to remaining shallow, self-centered, narcissistic beings.

I want you to see this point: Hard times bring about change, both on the inner and the outer. God uses them to develop a people of compassion, empathy, and love—those who can guide and help others. Hard times also create a point of reference. In the contrast and comparison between our former state and our present one, we can always remember *where* we were, *where* we came from, and recognize the gift of our current condition. For me, that serves as the basis of ongoing gratitude to the One who brought me through and has given me the life I have.

> *Weeping may linger for the night,*
> *but joy comes with the morning.*
> Psalm 30:5

On Clarity

clarity: n. The state, or measure of being clear, either in appearance, thought, or style.

I acted on an impulse, the results of which I find I am reveling in, not only today but probably for some time to come.

That time of the year has arrived. Sunny days and blue skies announced the advent of spring and, along with it, the beginning of a full-blown gardening season. The arrival of sunlight pouring through my windows also exposed their obvious dirty state.

I could not ignore the grime, though I didn't try to. My gardening business occupies most of my time and energy, and my work schedule doesn't list "washing windows at home" as a priority.

My computer desk sits next to the window in my front bedroom/office. The window's location creates the opportunity to view the daily arrival of morning. The scenes range from a blanket of fog to breathtaking sunrises.

Today, I find myself looking out the window and feeling pleased. I can see clearly. I could not say that yesterday.

I had plans for the day, more-or-less. I should have been preparing to head out to either mow a lawn or weed a garden for my clients. Instead, I found myself, without even giving any thought, taking the grimy blinds down. I filled the bathtub with hot, soapy water and plunked them in to soak.

I felt I couldn't do much to damage them, and improvement seemed like a reasonable possibility.

I grabbed a bottle of spray cleaner, an old toothbrush, and some Q-tips to scrub out the window tracks. Then I added a squeegee, rags, and a bucket of water to the cleaning arsenal as I began what felt like an attack mode.

The filth of both windows and blinds had bothered me for some time, so the aggressive action felt good. I scrubbed and washed the window on the inside and tackled the frames and tracks too. The scene improved a great deal, but I still had to deal with the exterior.

I needed to begin my gardening workday, but I was determined to deal with the screens and the outside when I returned. And I did!

First, I removed the screens, which enabled me to easily clean the windows. The screens had served as a collection point for dust, dirt, and pollution over quite a lengthy period of time. Their grungy state called for a good scrubbing with a brush and soapy water. After rinsing with the hose, I placed them back on the window and declared the task completed.

Back inside, I put the clean blinds in place. By then darkness had fallen, so I couldn't see the results of my efforts.

This morning, I find myself looking out the window, not for what I might see, but because I *can* see.

The word *clarity* comes to mind. Clarity was restored when I removed the dirt and grime from my window. I didn't have a flawed windowpane. However, the residue clouded it so much that my vision and view became clouded as well.

Often, much of our mind, lives, and inner vision match that same state. Layer upon layer of debris accumulates—so much that we experience impaired understanding, resulting in confusion. We wonder why we are taken by surprise when a current situation affects us, many times springboarding from earlier experiences. You know how that works. Stuff happens, and we just collect garbage, not that we want to, but because we can't seem to get rid of it. And, yes, that does affect the quality of the life we live here and now.

I am all for thorough cleaning, not only on the outer, but in the inner. Thankfully, my Heavenly Father is proficient when it comes to bringing about clarity.

Many years ago, He told me, "There is a better way." He doesn't mean a right way vs. a wrong way, but His way—a *better* way.

So if you find yourself in a place where you cannot deny a lot of muck and junk affects your life and clouds your ability to have clear insight, it might be a hint a thorough inner scrubbing is in order.

Living one's life in clarity *is* a better way to live. However, we cannot achieve it ourselves. Come before God in honesty and sincerity. He is able, capable, and willing.

Deep Cleaning

deep cleaning: n. Any thorough cleansing, especially one conducted in order to disinfect a place that has or may have been contaminated with a disease vector such as a virus, bacteria, etc.

I have begun a deep clean of my home, though I would call it more thorough than disinfectant. After years of tending the gardens and cleaning the homes of others, my turn has arrived. As a retiree, my workload has lessened. Hopefully, I will have both the time and energy to address the dirt and clutter throughout my own dwelling.

This project will not be one of those quick "Swiffer pass-through jobs." Nor will it fall in the category of dusting with "a lick-and-a-promise," as Mom directed on Sunday mornings when company had been invited for dinner after church.

"Leave no stone unturned" more aptly describes my mission as I go deep into corners that have not seen the light of day nor cleaning solution for years. I will pull out items and clean them before returning them to their home. I expect to make piles of things to keep, give away, or discard.

In preparation, I pulled the vacuum and cleaning supplies out of my truck, where I have stored them for years. When I had a cleaning job, having them readily available made sense. Plus, I didn't have to move the equipment in and out of my house.

I'm methodical about some things, such as how I address a job. When I cleaned a large garden area, I always began in the furthest corner and worked toward the house. I approached the "deep clean" in the same manner, starting in a corner of the living room, hidden behind the television, that no one sees or notices except me. The amount of filth that had accumulated amazed me.

A person experiences a real sense of accomplishment after doing something that has been left undone for quite some time. It "feels" good. This cleaning process won't reach completion in a few hours, a day, a week, or maybe even months. I will, however, go bit by bit until it's completed. I began today.

This physical deep clean reminds me of what God does spiritually. He begins in the most hidden crevices of our inner beings, those areas we don't want anyone to see or know about, most of all ourselves. As He pores into the deep, dark caverns within us, His very presence becomes like the head lantern on a spelunker. Secrets are revealed and, at His hand, dealt with one-at-a-time, one-on-one.

As with my home, a thorough inner cleaning takes a lengthy period of time. But the process and its end result are priceless *and* important. God's desire for us includes living in purity, a life unencumbered by garbage. A clean spiritual home is a better way. It is *His* way.

Search me, O God, and know my heart;
test me, and know my thoughts.
See if there is any wicked way in me,
and lead me in the way everlasting.
Psalm 139:23–24

On Seeing

see: v. To perceive or detect with the eyes; to view, observe, behold, to witness or observe by personal experience.

see: v. To form a mental picture of.
(figuratively) To understand.

The object lesson, which involved four socks, revealed itself before my eyes when I folded laundry. I paired two of them then, reaching for the other two, realized neither set matched. I looked at them when I picked them up but had not seen the obvious. The colors shouted a mismatch.

Have you ever had an experience where you looked but didn't see? Then you found the "invisible" item right in front of you, "as plain as the nose on your face," my mother would say. But somehow the visible image did not compute in your mind. How many times have your eyes passed over an object of search, perhaps a set of keys or that rogue tennis shoe your child needed in order to head off to school, or that important piece of paper you put in a special place for safekeeping? One would think if we were looking, we would see, but that doesn't always happen.

These types of incidents involve physical eyes. Another kind of sight exists, one of inner vision. Inner vision comes from our spiritual base and manifests in one having an awareness or knowledge far removed from the constraints of the material world. Some call it "having an epiphany, being enlightened," or "having an *aha* moment." Others would apply the description "getting it."

For me, this kind of seeing means I have insight, understanding without words, or have knowledge of or a grasp of spiritual concepts, truths, and precepts. Those revelations take place within my being. While they aren't visible to my physical eyes, as apparent as two sets of mismatched socks, they are solid and real, often life-changing.

Allow me to share what I see (now, isn't that an adroit application of the word?). Each of us falls into one of two categories at varying times in our lives. The first happens when we don't see what others see; the second converse category: seeing what others do not.

At times, scales cover our figurative eyes, leaving us with no ability to see the severity of our circumstances, the seriousness of our current state, or the dire straits of our actions and attitudes. We are blinded to ourselves.

While the end result of staying the course may shout, "*Disaster!*" as we head toward a cliff, we continue . . . because we don't see. Those around may observe and attempt to call attention and focus, but as a wise friend said, "If you don't see, you don't see."

In the second category *we* have sight, with a clear vision of another's state and alarming circumstances. In this situation, we can bump into a huge problem if not careful, that of judgment.

An easy assumption can follow: If things are obvious to *me*, then my friend, neighbor, spouse, child, should be able to discern those problem-causing areas as well. The trap of pointing a finger, harshly judging, and criticizing sits at the door, and we can readily fall into it. Surely these people we love and care for cannot help but see those things that are crystal clear to us. "Don't you see yourself?" we want to shout. However, if you don't see, you don't see.

Just as there have been plenty of times in my life when I didn't see myself, so it is for others. When I see what another does not, it is important I pray for them that they *might* see.

Be careful lest you judge others for things that are not clear to them, for things they do not see. Care for one another, and stand in support and understanding rather than judging.

God freely gives inner vision and sight—seeing. Never take a single God-given revelation lightly. Hold on to each one. He gives them to bring about inner change, growth, and maturity.

When I do see myself, perhaps in a figurative mirror, I can no longer plead ignorance or denial. The truth of self has no escape door. I have no excuse and am held personally accountable. The responsibility for my life, my choices, and my actions fall on my doorstep.

> *"I see," said the blind man.*
> Anonymous

> *"Therefore I advise you to buy from me . . .*
> *salve to anoint your eyes so that you may see."*
> Revelation 3:18

On Unbelief

unbelief: n. An absence of belief.

belief: n. Mental acceptance of a claim as true. Faith or trust in the reality of something; often based upon one's own reasoning, trust in a claim, desire of actuality, and/or evidence considered.

I wonder if he knows I'm the one who feeds him.

I heard him before I saw him. I've learned to recognize the click-clicking sound of my resident hummingbird. He frequents a feeder filled with sugar water hanging on my back patio. Many hummers feed while poised midair, beating their wings. This little guy plants himself on the perch of the feeder and guzzles away, often for long periods at a time.

Today, while I dug in the soil, seeking renewal of my mind and spirit, he sat like a sentinel atop the highest branch of the nearby lilac bush. Typically, hummingbirds appear to be in a nonstop flight mode, vaguely resembling miniature bombers as they flap their wings up to four thousand times per minute. Not so this little guy. He knows how to have his "down" time.

When claustrophobia takes hold, I head for the outdoors and fresh air. Winter has just officially started, but weeds have already begun to cover any bare soil with bright green vegetation. Several industrial-sized garbage bags filled with leaves waited to be spread on my garden. It was late in the day and quite cool. Dressed in warm clothes, I responded to my garden's beckoning.

These kinds of tasks create the opportunity for hands-and-knees kind of thinking. No one interrupts, and the mindless work frees up my mind for thought. The moist soil allowed the weeds to come out easily. I cleared an area to stack with leaves that would compost, enriching the soil.

Periodically I glanced up and noted my feathered friend still sat on his observation post. Occasionally, he did dash away to some very important appointment but quickly returned to his station. When I'm in this pensive frame of mind, I don't keep track of time. It was just God and me, and the hummingbird made three.

I have carried a heavy heart recently. Relief and peace evade me in these troubling times. Worries and inner turmoil plague me as I seek the "peace of God, which surpasses all understanding."[15]

The hummingbird's presence served as a reminder: "Look at the birds of the air; they do not sow or reap or store away in barns, and yet your heavenly Father feeds them. Are you not much more valuable than they?"[16] I cannot deny the love and care God has given me throughout my life. He deserves far more trust and respect than I give Him.

As darkness approached, I gathered my tools. *"Help my unbelief,"* my heart cried as I went inside to the welcoming warmth. The hummer flew off to settle down for the night as well.

---

[15] Philippians 4:7

[16] Matthew 6:26 NIV

Christ's public ministry on earth lasted three years. It began with His ordination by the Holy Spirit when John baptized Him. It ended with His crucifixion, resurrection, and ascension into heaven.

During this time, He called twelve to walk with Him. These ordinary men left their lives and families to follow Him and to be taught. They became part of an extraordinary event taking place right in front of them, one that would be chronicled as a pivotal point in the history of humanity.

The Scriptures talk about Peter, James, and John going with Christ to a mountaintop. There, God Himself verified Christ as His beloved Son when Jesus visibly changed into His heavenly form before their eyes.

Masses of people followed Christ wherever He went during His time of ministry. While the four were on the mountain, a crowd formed below and waited. Part of the large throng included a father who brought his demon-possessed son to be healed. I cannot imagine the heartache and disappointment he experienced as he went from the highest hope to the lowest low when none of the other disciples there could free the young man. In that emotional devastation, doubt most certainly overwhelmed him.

When Jesus came down from the mountaintop, the father told Him of the circumstances in his young boy's life: An evil spirit caused his son to be deaf and mute, brought seizures, and tried to destroy him by casting him into fire or water. He begged Jesus for help. "All things can be done for the one who believes," Jesus responded.

As tears rolled down his face, the dad cried out, "I believe; help my unbelief!" With that, Jesus rebuked the foul spirit and ordered it to come out of the child and never enter again.[17]

My recent life resembles that of a yo-yo. Up, down. Up, down. As a person of faith, I do know in my heart nothing that happens can be separate from God, including the here and now. However, I can totally relate to that father and his dichotomy, the appearance of a contradiction of faith.

How can I believe and still have unbelief?

Doubt is the leavening of unbelief. It may come in a torrential flood or silently move in like a stifling fog. The underlying goal of doubt, to challenge the validity and strength of one's faith, never varies. Care must be taken to keep doubt outside the door instead of allowing it to walk in and take up residence.

Nothing magical takes place when we choose to live life with God. Often, we must dig deep within ourselves, grinding out the nitty-gritty of things. Unbelief falls in that category. Its presence cannot be willed away by mind power and needs to be dealt with, by God and in His presence.

"I do believe. Help my unbelief."

I am at His mercy. As are you.

By the way, I read that hummingbirds do recognize people. They are territorial, and I want to believe my resident hummer knows I am the one who feeds him. God gifted him to me, a personal "support animal," as two very different types of gardens were dealt with, my outer physical garden as well as my inner.

I am blessed.

---

[17] Mark 9:17–27

On Cloud Covers, Vision, and Faith

cloud: n. A visible mass of water droplets suspended in the air. Anything that makes things foggy or gloomy

I have an image in my mind's eye. I can easily relate to the mental picture, as the scene occurs quite often in the Pacific Northwest where I live. The weather people describe the condition as a "cloud cover." During certain times of the year, the cover becomes quite thick and takes the form of fog. With regularity, we Oregon earthlings must deal with not only limited but nonexistent visibility.

In my mind I look upward and see only clouds. I know if I could visually penetrate them an endless scope would open. But my physical limitations bind me to this sphere called Earth. I cannot see beyond the clouds.

I know a woman whose mother passed recently. She had been ill for quite some time, but her passing, nonetheless, created a source of pain and grief for the family. This past Thanksgiving marked a first holiday without their mother and grandmother. Now, with Christmas coming, they must deal with another inevitable first. The reality and experience of loss often fills the heart with sorrow.

A man spoke with me yesterday about the death of his best friend. He said he will grieve his passing for the rest of his life. His friend had also been sick with a terminal illness, and the friend's death was no shock. Even so he, too, faces the holiday with a sense of loss—deep, personal loss.

Why? Why does such pain and grief exist in our lives? At times the heartaches seem never-ending, the same song playing over and over. The circumstances, scenery, and calendar appear to be the only things that change.

For some, sorrow becomes a debilitating factor in living life. For others the pain and hurt overpower and consume. The holiday season, Thanksgiving and Christmas, often only intensify and amplify the grief.

I have no answer as to the "why" of things, particularly in the lives of others. I possess limited spiritual vision in the same way a cloud cover curtails my physical view. Any insights I may have happen when I am allowed to see from above, as it were . . . to see as God sees.

The dictionary describes faith as "something that is believed especially with strong conviction" and "a firm belief in something for which there is no proof."[18] My simple description of faith: I believe even though I do not see.

A common point of view prevails that only those who exercise a belief in God live a life of faith. But all humankind lives a faith-based life. The difference between the two lies in the object of that faith. Some have chosen to place their faith in a Person, an Entity, One with personality and intrinsic love. Others place their faith in theories, hypotheses, suppositions, ideologies, or self. While the two are polar opposites, the strength of belief is identical.

---

[18] *Merriam-Webster Dictionary*, https://www.merriam-webster.com/dictionary/faith, accessed February 15, 2025.

I had a favorite aunt whose only child was born with Down syndrome. She and my uncle lived their lives in total dedication to the love and care of my cousin. I never remember hearing them complain over their lot in life. I do remember the love bestowed upon Bonnie.

One single comment from my aunt remains within me to this day. After a family get-together, the women in the kitchen must have been discussing faith. Very, very quietly she said, "Sometimes you don't understand. You just have to have faith." And she said no more. She walked the walk.

I believe all circumstances carry a divine point and purpose, even the difficult and heartbreaking ones. Living life with God means entrusting my life to the One who created and designed me. And much of the time without answers or understanding.

Seeing beyond the spiritual cloud cover with true vision is a gift from God. To us. For us.

Revel in every one of the glimpses, insights, and truths He gives. Each is a building block of great importance in life, revelations from God Himself. Those personal treasures become part of you as you live out your life — pillars of truth within your being.

For we walk by faith, not by sight.
2 Corinthians 5:7

On Being Grounded

grounded: adj. Confined to stay inside, typically by a parent, as a punishment; in aviation, not allowed to fly. Well-balanced and sensible.

discipline: v. Train (someone) to obey rules or a code of behavior; using punishment to correct disobedience.

Mom and Dad delivered the verdict to the almost-thirteen-year-old: "You're grounded!" As her punishment, she had to choose between missing out on a friend's birthday party or relinquishing her cell phone for thirty days. She, along with her group of friends, had anticipated the ice-skating party for days. However, the prospect of giving up her phone, the social connection and lifeline for a preteen, for thirty *whole* days felt daunting.

She did not have cruel and abusive parents. They set a standard of honesty and forthrightness in their household. When she didn't meet that standard, consequences followed.

For many generations, a common form of discipline for children consisted largely of corporal punishment. A parent or an authority figure, perhaps even a teacher or coach, often caused physical pain or discomfort to a minor child who displayed undesirable behavior. They struck the child on his/her bottom with an open hand or an implement such as a paddle, deemed "the board of education" by some. Fear of the punishment, which would hopefully deter any future miscreant conduct, served as the base premise for this approach.

In my own life, Mom had a wooden paint-stirring stick as her paddle. When I pushed her beyond frustration, Dad took over when he got home from work. I imagine the final straw occurred when I ran from her to avoid the spanking, putting my hands behind my back to protect my behind.

Dad literally took me to the woodshed, where he paddled me with his bare hand. The size of his hand seemed enormous. While I have no doubt this involved pain, I don't remember ever feeling the punishment was undeserved. I always knew my actions warranted a response from my parents. My sassy mouth and the need to have the last word probably brought the discipline.

Children enter a family and home with a blank slate. Parents or guardians bear the responsibility of nurturing and guiding them, training and teaching the values and principles that will serve as a moral compass and spiritual foundation for their children throughout their lives.

In the home children learn, both from example and daily experience, how to interact with others. In that safe space, they are taught the difference between acceptable and unacceptable behavior. They also come to understand the importance and meaning of discipline. Everyday incidents provide teaching tools to encourage development, maturity, and the growth of self-control.

The form of punishment for children has undergone a transition over the past several decades. Grounding, the restriction placed on a child from an activity or favorite object, has become a preferred method used in discipline and training, instead of exacting both physical and emotional pain by means of spanking, for example.

God represents the epitome of a loving parent. A clear correlation can be drawn between that of earthly parents and our Heavenly Father.

The Innovator and Master of instruction, He utilizes everyday life to teach us a better way to live. At times the experiences become quite difficult and harsh, but only because of our bullheadedness and refusal to work with Him and allow Him into our lives. We often ignore wake-up calls and leave Him no other option than to apply more pressure.

God operates in the long-term, not short-term. He wants only the best for us and does not choose a crunch situation as His first option. However, if stubbornness rears its head, we leave Him with no alternative. His tough love comes from the base: *"If there was any other way . . . Eternity is a long, long time."*

In aviation a grounded pilot has their flying privileges revoked. That same term applied by God simply means I have "clipped wings." He places me in a set of circumstances I have not chosen — nor particularly like. That process reshapes the life *I* had planned. The experience can manifest in an infinite number of ways: as mundane as weather conditions delaying a trip or a fender-bender in a parking lot. It might be as dramatic as the alteration of retirement plans because of an illness, a stock market shift that results in financial losses, or a natural disaster, just to name a few.

As a young woman, I had life as a mother all planned. I decided my family would be complete with two children, and *I* would determine when that would happen. Nothing went as I intended. God introduced Himself to me in one of my early adult experiences by grounding me when infertility ruled my life. Eventually, I realized He simply did not allow me to have my way. In His way and in His time, He blessed me with four children. And that sums up the point and purpose of discipline at the hand of God. His way *is* a better way.

I questioned my grandgirl about her grounding experience. I asked if she felt the punishment was effective and what she learned from it. "I have never lied since," she said. "I do feel that it taught me something. It taught me a lesson to never lie, always tell the truth, because lying can get you in trouble, can hurt someone's feelings."

Mom and Dad's grounding appears to have made its point. The thirty days my grandgirl had no phone served as a constant reminder of her unacceptable behavior.

The terms discipline and punishment have such negative undercurrents attached to them in today's society that those in charge have a reluctance to apply them. However, when they come from a base of love and wisdom, nothing can replace their value or necessity.

If you discover you are grounded, remember this: grounding at His hand results in one becoming grounded. Everything in life has a point and purpose, even discipline. And you may quote me on that.

> *It is never fun to be corrected.*
> *In fact, at the time it is always painful.*
> *But if we learn to obey by being corrected,*
> *we will do right and live at peace.*
> Hebrews 12:11 CEV

Hearing vs. Listening

hear: v. To perceive sounds through the ear.

listen: v. To pay attention to a sound or speech.

There is hearing. And then there is listening.

Many years ago, a wise person told me, "Listening is an art." Nodding my head in agreement, I smiled, feigning comprehension and understanding. In truth, as a "talker" I didn't have even the vaguest idea of what she meant. Since then, I have learned not only the importance and value of listening but *how* to listen.

Have you ever been in a conversation with someone and realized they turned a deaf ear when you spoke? Perhaps you sensed the lack of interest as their eyes wandered. You may have noted their distraction and absence of focus as they waited, or maybe even interrupted you, to speak of the things that mattered to *them*. They may have heard, but they did not listen. You had the choice of either entering into a verbal competition or turning silent. Then, as the visit ended, the real sense remained that neither you nor what you had to say mattered.

Something inexplicably cathartic takes place within a person when another human listens, giving them voice, allowing them to be fully heard. This seems to be particularly apparent for one coping with a difficult situation or set of circumstances. Often, objectivity takes place as they reveal personal details. A new perspective may also come into play. Things don't feel as monumental, overwhelming, or consuming. They lose their sting.

No price tag can be placed on the experience of being given the freedom to express yourself. Actually, the mental health field with its therapists, psychiatrists, and psychologists focus on that kind of self-expression.

The art of listening shouldn't be reserved exclusively for friends and family. Opportunities for listening abound and include encounters with all types of people in everyday life — at the grocery store, the gas station, or the gym — at work and outside of work. In my experience these interactions usually involve individuals I don't know and will never see again.

Very personal things may be shared, from one stranger to another. Respect those revelations with confidence. As a friend says, "Lock them up inside." Even though a personal relationship may not be involved, a baring of the soul deserves respect. Most of the time people don't expect an answer or solution — they do have a need to be heard and listened to.

How does one become a listener? I feel setting self aside meets the requirements for a basic first step. If telling *my* story, *my* experiences, *my* thoughts and ideas become my main concern, then I will never really listen. At first, it takes a conscious effort to push self aside and just listen. Patience matters as well. If I am rushed, the impatience shouts. The unspoken message I give: "I don't have time for you."

Most people simply need a sounding board and don't even realize it. The desire to be listened to, from the youngest to the eldest, runs deep within humankind. The unspoken requirement for affirmation that "I am of worth. I matter" covers a broad swath of humanity

I end with a challenge: If you aren't already a listener, try becoming one. Set self aside. Ask questions. I think you will be surprised at some of the responses you receive as well as the effect they may have on your own life. You will certainly create the potential of making a difference in the life of another. Just listen.

On Things

thing: n. A material object without life or consciousness; an inanimate object.

The sturdy wooden dresser belonged to a bedroom set passed on to me by my parents after they purchased a replacement set when they moved into the "new house." Seventy-three years later the chiffonier, the term always used in its description, continues serving purpose in my home, storing articles of clothing.

As a child, I collected and "saved." The top drawer of the dresser contained my life's treasures. It held a shoebox filled with napkins garnered from every event I attended. This included weddings, church functions, family get-togethers, gatherings, and meals at restaurants. Often, they displayed the name of the couple getting married or those celebrating a momentous anniversary. If not, I wrote the date, the occasion, and location on them as I tucked them away. The small pieces of folded paper, including one of rice paper, comprised the diary of a young girl's social life.

The drawer also held the accumulation of another collection—pencils. They carried the inscription of a business or company name and served as an advertisement for them. I never sharpened a single one and stored them in a cigar box that fit perfectly in the top drawer.

A stash of plastic Dairy Queen spoons completed the

assortment. I can't recall why they held such a place of value and importance for me. However, after a Sunday evening treat on the way home from church, I felt compelled to wash each plastic spoon with its trademark curl on the end of the handle and place it in my drawer along with the others. The collection was impressive.

My collections, an assortment of unimportant "things" certainly had no monetary value. But at that point in my life, they mattered. I left them behind when I married. Later, I disposed of them, but not without some inner turmoil and angst. Letting go of the things from one's past actually means letting go *of* that past. That process can be difficult as emotions come into play. The outcome, however, can free a person.

Several years ago, I experienced circumstances that resulted in downsizing, an innocuous term. In truth, that word describes getting rid of things that take up space and are, perhaps, no longer needed. Downsizing, however, may also entail giving up items that carry with them a deep, emotional connection. As I let go of many of my material possessions, I realized how little I actually need in order to live life. The process proved to be a huge step for a collector and saver. The aftermath became one of the most liberating experiences of my life.

Consider, if you will, all the time, energy, and money we humans expend taking care of our "things." We collect, protect, insure, display, and flaunt them. And, many times, categorize and organize them. Often, we spend a great deal of *our* life caring for them in the attempt to extend *their* life. (My 1997 Ford Ranger pickup fell in that category.)

Some hoard their things. Others sell them for a profit. And do not forget those who constantly compare *their* things with those of their neighbors, friends, or family. Many spend their lives making certain they get the best deal for the best "thing." That kind of focus can become a taxing, consuming, obsessive lifestyle.

Several years ago, "keeping up with the Joneses" described the rivalry regarding "things"—all expressed in the saying, "He who dies with the most toys wins."

Many families divide and split to shreds when the estate of a deceased family member goes into settlement. The sources of dispute can range from a memento to an heirloom, property, or money. Oftentimes, relationships become irreparably damaged and sacrificed, all for the sake of wanting to be the one who ends up possessing things deemed valuable.

"We don't own the things; the things own us" aptly describes life for many.

And yet in the end, no one ever has, or ever will, take a single "thing" with them when they leave this earth. No matter how much time, energy, and money we invest in the care and protection of our things, the final outcome never changes. "We came into this world with nothing. For sure, when we die, we will take nothing with us," 1 Timothy 6:7.

Perhaps now would be a good time to evaluate priorities.

People matter. Spiritual health and well-being matter. The things money cannot buy matter, including a relationship with God Himself. Those constitute priceless, invaluable treasures, the ones worth having.

Stop. Take a long look in the mirror. Where do you invest your time, your life, and your money? Make those investments count.

> *And he said to them, "Take care!*
> *Be on your guard against all kinds of greed,*
> *for one's life does not consist*
> *in the abundance of possessions."*
> Luke 12:15

On Storing Junk

junk: n. Discarded or waste material; rubbish, trash. A collection of miscellaneous items of little value.

I made a trip yesterday to the cosmetic section of the local department store for a makeover—although that word itself is a *long* stretch of the imagination. When someone with experience applies your makeup, that doesn't even qualify as a "redo," let alone a makeover. The makeup representative wanted to know how she could help me. I asked if she could start by taking off twenty years. Apparently, they don't sell that. I did come home with some new makeup, though, and no place to store it.

My bathroom has plenty of drawers for storage and, as a single person, only my own items to house. I found them, however, filled with junk. As I began dumping and sorting, I discovered things I didn't know I had, items I will never use. I found junk, pure junk.

Why? Why did I have empty containers, old toothbrushes, ancient perfume, and outdated makeup? Why did I store so much junk? Probably because shoving stuff in a drawer seems easier than dealing with it. "Out of sight, out of mind."

As I carried a large bag of trash to the garbage can, I thought about how easily I eliminated the junk from my bathroom drawers. My thoughts went from there to the junk we all store within ourselves. Getting rid of inner junk is not so easy, yet more important than dealing with any physical junk we may be storing.

We all have, or have had, things we carry around internally. Our current society uses the generic description "issues." Whatever term you might use, including baggage, stuff, or junk, it's all the same. The clutter serves no purpose and takes up as much valuable space within a person as old toothbrushes did in my drawer. Holding on to the stuff stifles one's growth, both spiritually and emotionally.

Why *do* we hold on to this personal junk? Probably the same reason as in the physical. Pushing all the garbage into a drawer, albeit an inner, figurative one, seems easier than facing it and doing something about it.

However, by the very definition of junk, it *is* junk. The more we possess, the less ability we have to live life well. Junk taints and poisons our inner beings with its toxicity.

What, exactly, defines inner junk? Perhaps a relationship fell apart, but a person cannot get rid of the emotion and pain. Others might be unwilling to let go of a personal affront. Maybe you, your child, or another family member were treated unfairly at school or work, and you can't let it go. The possible situations have no end. The longer we hold onto any unpleasant facet of an experience, the more harmful the effect within us. Left unaddressed, the state never improves. A negative never changes and will *always* have a negative effect within us.

Compare this situation to a rock thrown into water. The concentric circles that move out touch other areas of our lives. Unresolved, the initial incident grows and grows, eventually enveloping the whole of our being, creating an environment that stifles any semblance of health, be it emotional, spiritual, or mental.

Getting rid of junk is not easy. And yet it is.

Personally, I decided to live unencumbered by all the junk. I then asked God to clean out my inner being. I didn't want to look at myself in light and truth, so that made the process difficult at times. The end results delight me, though.

The removal of inner junk is well worth it, and one I highly recommend. God does good work, the best kind of makeover.

On Creatures of Habit

habit: n. An action performed on a regular basis. An action performed repeatedly and automatically, usually without awareness.

I made the switch more than a week ago. I wouldn't categorize the change as earth-shattering or life-changing. I simply interchanged the microwave and toaster when I realized they would then each be more efficiently located. The move appears to be a good one, if such an appraisal can be applied to kitchen appliances. However, I was gobsmacked once again this morning, though, to realize I am undeniably a creature of habit.

Unconsciously, without thought, I headed toward the toaster, the former location of the microwave, with my teacup to heat the water. I could say I hadn't quite awakened, since the sun hadn't yet risen, but such occurrences seem to be happening regularly. Just last night I reached for the microwave with the bread I planned to toast. I cannot tell you how many times I've looked in the direction of the toaster expecting to see the time on the microwave's digital clock.

Habits fill our lives, whether asleep or awake. If I actually considered how much they factor into daily living, my head would take to spinning in place. For example, since my mind has gone in that direction, I realized I put my socks on in a certain order, left foot first. I always leave doors open when I go outside, a consequence of locking myself out once. Without any doubt, these unconscious acts permeate my life.

Watch and see what happens if we cannot do something heretofore ingrained in our daily lives. It may be as simple as having to adjust to another time zone while traveling or coping with the time change for daylight saving time. Try altering your personal "first-thing-in-the-morning" pattern and see how uncomfortable life becomes. And, if you really want to see what happens, rearrange the toaster and microwave in the kitchen.

The loss of a loved one or a catastrophic event, which affects all routine, can alter a person's life permanently. For some, it carries the potential to be disastrous, as one's familiar world turns upside-down, propelling folk into the fetal position.

Daily rituals, patterns, order, and routine. In truth, these habits monitor how, when, and where we live our lives. I think comfort and a semblance of control must be present in the sameness of things and the repetition of life. They create a rhythm of sort, an attempt to minimize the surprises in our lives.

As humans, we tend to define habits in our lives as either good habits or bad habits. The bad ones include those things we do not like about ourselves and want to change. In my own life, procrastination fits that description. The good ones counter the degradation and demeaning of self with behavior that makes us feel truly wonderful about ourselves. For example, I always make sure I fold my towels with the hemmed edges inside. Pretty silly, right? Remove those labels of good and bad. I believe many of our behaviors are traits that make us unique individuals, the idiosyncrasies that identify each of us as one-of-a-kind.

Some say that in order to break a habit, and that would, of course, be a "bad" habit, one need only substitute the behavior with another for two weeks. Of course, the replacement would be a "good" habit. Others suggest it takes thirty to sixty days or even longer.

Now, it might just be me, but I've tried that approach more than once and find it to be short-term. Before I know it, I'm back in the old habit pattern I had hoped to change. Hence, I have a strong conviction that, left to myself, "old habits die hard." They really do, especially when the implementation of death is in my hands.

For the most part, I have given up trying to change myself. I find it an exercise in futility. Thus, I leave personal change in the hands of my Heavenly Father.

True change must be the goal, I think—becoming a different person, a different *kind* of person, not just altering one's habits. To change only a habit is akin to using a Band-Aid on an internal injury.

I speak of real, valid, undeniable, irreversible change that takes place within a person instead of just altering an action:

- Peace, not tension
- Contentment in place of discontent
- Courage instead of fear
- Joy replacing depression
- Gentleness, not harshness
- Generosity as opposed to selfishness
- Kindness instead of unkindness

- Harmony rather than discord
- Love, not hate

Only God can accomplish that. As the saying goes, "God loves me as I am, but He loves me too much to leave me that way."

Yes, we *are* creatures of habit in so many ways. But we don't have to carry the burden of trying to change ourselves where and when it really matters. There is One who is able, capable, and willing to do that.

And sooner or later I'll figure out I can't heat my tea water in the toaster or toast my bread in the microwave.

"Old habits die hard."

On Looking Back

A basic fact exists: It is physically impossible to look forward and backward at the same time. It cannot be done. A person can see one direction or the other, but the eyes can't take in both at once.

The same fact applies to one's inner vision. When you spend time focusing on the past, living it over and over again with guilt, regret, and "if only," you expend all your energy there. The past becomes your home, your dwelling place. You live there—stuck in the past.

The result resembles being sucked down into a whirlpool. As you spin in circles, its force renders you powerless and immobile with no chance or hope of ever getting out and moving forward.

While letting go of one's past may seem easier said than done, hanging on to it weighs a person down in the most literal sense. The past becomes a heavy burden to carry, with no real payoffs, unless you've made qualifying for martyrdom your goal. God's plan and desire for us emphasizes living in the present. Setting up residence in the past serves no purpose.

Living in the present, ever moving forward, occupies a place of importance in order to live a viable, productive, complete, and satisfying life. How do I know? I come from a place of experience. My Creator taught me this as a first lesson.

Valuable principles like these establish a foundation, the base for other building blocks in a person's life. In my opinion, this one holds a place of great benefit and worth.

But I focus on this one thing:
Forgetting the past
and looking forward to what lies ahead.
Philippians 3:13 NLT

On Prayer: Just Ask with Your Heart

prayer: n. a practice of communicating with one's God; the specific words or methods used for praying

What, exactly, is prayer? How *do* you pray? Does "it" work? And another question: Why bother?

Prayer can be described as the simple act of talking with, and to, God one-on-one. You either practice praying . . . or you don't. You either believe in the importance and value of prayer, or you may view it as something only the weak, naïve, and feeble-minded engage in—although when times get really tough, more than one such person has thrown a Hail Mary prayer to a God they don't even give credence to. It could be said, "Desperate times call for desperate measures." You might also be one who has never considered prayer or God to serve any earthly purpose, so the idea of praying has never entered your mind.

Communicating with God serves as an important part of daily life for people of faith. Personally, prayer saturates my being every day as my spirit and soul reach out to my Heavenly Father. We all have needs and concerns, worries and problems. God says we may bring those to Him and leave them at His feet. Some requests come from a private place. Other pleas are on behalf of family and friends. Many people make a point of including those they don't personally know and have never met when they pray.

How *does* one pray? God has no rules, limitations, or boundaries. When one has a best friend, a no-holds-barred friend, and that friend knows all your secrets and every single thing about you, you are free. Free to be yourself.

For some, prayer may be like a meal where a person stops and eats, as they set aside a specific time to communicate with God. For others, prayer might be likened to a visit to the emergency room, a last resort utilized only in the most dire and crucial times of life.

What should I do? Help! Thank You SO much! I don't understand. What is the point? I don't get it. I am scared — really, really scared. Are You sure You know what You're doing?

Much of my communication with God consists of this kind of open, unencumbered honesty. And, yes, this *is* prayer. Do I ask specific things of Him as well? Absolutely!

I had a dream the other night. In my dream, a young woman and I shared a conversation about prayer. She didn't speak openly about her spiritual life, but she had either prayed *for* someone or *about* something. Soft-spoken and with reticence, she very quietly said, "I just asked with my heart."

Words do not matter when it comes to prayer. One's heart and sincerity make the difference. Prayer can be summarized as personal, private communication for God's ears only, as you reach out, seeking Him and Him alone. Just ask with your heart.

As to whether or not "it" works, I feel that comes with several caveats. The power of prayer depends upon whom one prays to, one's relationship to and with that entity, and the resources available to that being. The One I pray to has unlimited resources and wholeheartedly desires to share them.

And that brings me to the final question. Why bother?

On my best of days, I can barely see the nose on the end of my face. I live and function at ground level. Left to myself, I flounder without direction. Why, then, wouldn't I spend time with the One who knows me far better than I know myself? The One who loves me and cares about every facet of my life. The One who created the world and everything in it. Prayer is my lifeline—to God and to my sanity.

My God lives. He bears no resemblance to a fabricated mogul that demands subservience, nor those many gods whose images are created from stone. When I reach out to Him, He hears. He listens. And He responds.

And *that* is the most important reason of all.

> *"Come to me, all you who are weary*
> *and are carrying heavy burdens,*
> *and I will give you rest."*
> Matthew 11:28

On Contentment

contentment: n. Quality or state of being content.

content: adj. In a state of satisfaction; satisfied about a particular circumstance.

The sun shone brightly, with a hint of warmth even. The thermometer registered 50 degrees, a welcome change from the freezing rain, ice storm, snow, and icy roads that plagued my area for the past month. My client had scheduled me to clean her house, but she directed me to her backyard instead.

Raised beds filled the entire space. She gardens year-round, and winter greens packed several of them. She instructed me to weed and remove leaves damaged by the freeze then deal with a bed of strawberries. As I methodically worked my way around the beds with pruners and a weeding tool, the thought struck me: *This is where I am most at peace.*

I am my father's daughter, a farmer's daughter. Perhaps I have been in a state of denial. The description seems so "earthy," so unglamorous without a single hint of sophistication. And yet the term suits me perfectly. "A farmer's daughter" characterizes exactly what and who I am.

I feel "at home" outdoors, working alone. You'll find me as comfortable on my hands and knees, digging in the dirt, as when I sit at my piano. Contentment fills my being.

What, exactly, is contentment, and how can it be found?

For some, contentment may remain elusive while they search or strive for someone or something to bring about a sense of being settled, at peace, of "feeling good." Their life may be in a constant upheaval, as though on a carousel, going round and round, up and down with the scenery never changing in the quest.

Consider little children. Most families have had *that* Christmas morning gifting experience. After all the thought, time, and money invested in choosing the "perfect" gift for a child, the little one finds an empty box and becomes completely entertained and enthralled. They crawl in and out of the cardboard haven. They may place it over their head. After piling bows or wrapping paper in their new-found source of entertainment, they dump everything out and start all over again.

That is contentment. It comes from within, with no thought beyond the moment, no cares or concerns for what tomorrow might bring. Either we are, or we aren't . . . content, that is.

Take children to a creek or the beach in the summertime, and they will spend hours creating channels and dams with the wet sand or dirt. They might collect precious treasures of beautiful rocks or shells or use chunks of wood as a shovel. The discovery of insects or frogs becomes a mesmerizing experience. (Oh, how the tears fall when time runs out and the one in charge tells them they have to leave it all behind.) *That* illustrates contentment as they simply live life. These kinds of experiences cannot be measured in monetary terms.

Sometimes I wonder if the concept of contentment ever enters the minds of most people as they search for success or importance in the current hurried, frenetic state in our society. Humans often resemble ants in an anthill, ever moving at a great rate of speed, each in their own direction, crawling over one another with abandon. They never really pay attention to those around them or their own inner state. "Going nowhere fast" describes the condition perfectly.

Many in life do find contentment, however, through their families. For some, living out a calling, dedicated to an important cause or purpose may also provide that fulfillment. Others may have a career or employment that provides a sense of deep satisfaction.

I cannot speak for anyone else, only myself. Personally, having a friendship with my Creator and living my life in a spiritual manner has resulted in contentment. As I compare current experiences with those in my past, I see acceptance of the day-to-day events of my life has been a natural consequence in the context of that relationship.

Do I live my life in a nirvana state of peace, tranquility, happiness, and contentment? No. I do not, but I *am* a work in progress.

Contentment can most certainly be called a priceless gift. It behaves like a rhythmic, steady heartbeat that courses through one's being, never altering or changing. May each of you be blessed with contentment in your own lives.

I have learned, in whatever state I am, to be content.
Philippians 4:11 RSV

There is great gain in godliness with contentment.
1 Timothy 6:6 RSV

On Injury, Healing, and Scars

injury: n. Damage to the body of a human or animal.

healing: n. The process where the cells in the body regenerate and repair themselves. The psychological process of dealing with a problem or problems.

scar: n. A permanent mark on the skin sometimes caused by the healing of a wound. A permanent mark on the mind.

My eyes caught the tiny scar as I glanced at my ankle. I hadn't noticed it or thought about the event that caused it in years. I was no more than four years old when a stack of lumber fell over, trapping my foot, the weight of the 2x4s damaging it. Seventy-plus years later, I carry the reminder of the incident on my body.

My older brother had been assigned the task of piling the lumber so it would be ready for our father to continue the construction of a new family home after he completed his day job at a local plywood mill. I was most certainly uninvited help. The outcome verified that.

Physical scars create a personal record that we carry on our bodies. They mark periods of time and events in our lives, each one with its own unique story. Mine carries the evidence of more than a few stitches that have faded with time. During elementary school, I made an annual trip to the doctor when a gash or an open wound required sutures. Some may wear the aftermath of a dreadful bicycle accident, a painful burn, a surgical procedure, or a stumble into an unforgiving brick hearth or a heavy wooden coffee table. The list of possibilities has no end. I suspect humankind worldwide shares the experience of possessing a physical scar of some sort.

First, the injury. Then the healing. Often, visible scars remain. They serve as reminders, sometimes gentle, other times stark, of where we were and what we were doing at an exact point in time. Perhaps they may point to the reality of protection and being spared further harm as well. "It could have been worse."

Another type of injury exists besides physical injury. The experiences that affect one emotionally cannot be seen by the naked eye. The potential for enveloping bitterness and permanent internal scarring can easily manifest. Hurt, anger, dismay, or great angst may flourish in a person's inner breeding ground, promoting infection in one's soul.

Who among us hasn't engaged in an argument with a spouse, friend, coworker, or even a stranger where hurtful words dominated the exchange? Have those of you reading this become part of a situation where the trauma of illness, dementia, or an accident takes over and consumes not only the patient but family and friends as well? Divorce or a bitter end to a relationship often bring out the worst in people, where the children become pawns and victims. Inner injuries can develop when a partner or best friend dies. Likewise, having to stand by helplessly while witnessing the self-destruction of a child. On and on and on . . .

This kind of injury does not heal so readily as physical trauma. Cell regeneration does not take place. Bandages, splints, stitches, and antibiotics are ineffective. My personal confirmation, however: Restoration is possible as the pain lessens while healing takes place, all at the hand of God as we come to Him in our helpless, damaged state.

The Bible talks about Christ appearing to his disciples after His crucifixion and resurrection. Questions and doubts filled their minds. They did not receive Him with open arms. "Put your finger here, and see my hands; and put out your hand, and place it in my side; do not be faithless, but believing,"[19] He told a doubting Thomas. Following Christ's instructions, noting the places where those who crucified Him nailed His hands to the cross and thrust the sword into His side, Thomas responded, "My Lord and my God."[20]

The physical body of Christ endured excruciating injury as He became our sacrifice, bearing the weight of our condemnation. He wears those scars.

A friend told me of a dream/experience, my term for occurrences while sleeping that go beyond a dream state. These cannot be casually passed off as a "figment of one's imagination." They qualify as experience because they involve one's whole being.

My friend lived with the fear that Jesus would return and he would reject Him because he did not recognize Him. One night, Christ appeared to him in his sleep and held out His hands—in the same way He did with Thomas. Immediately, my friend saw the scars on Jesus's hands and *knew*. Doubt disappeared. The fear no longer haunts him.

---

[19] John 20:27 RSV
[20] John 20:28 RSV

Why does Christ still carry those scars? Why didn't His body become "perfect" upon His resurrection and in His glorified state? I do not know.

Regardless of status, race, or citizenship, humankind shares the common experience of injury. An old adage states that time heals all wounds, and for many that rings true. For others, however, healing never takes place as it remains elusive, ever just out of reach. My desire and prayer: that each of you know healing at the hand of God, in both the inner and the outer.

And may you own your physical scars with acceptance and pride. Know that they represent the completion of the process of injury and healing, with the scar a period on the end of your story. The scars on Christ's body certainly represent that, as He spoke from the cross: "It is finished."[21]

There is a point and purpose to everything.

O LORD my God, I cried to thee for help, and thou hast healed me.
Psalm 30:2 RSV

---

[21] John 19:30

On Grievances and Healing

grievance: n. Something that causes grief; a wrong or hardship suffered, which is the ground of a complaint.

The thorn finally came to the surface of my flesh so I could easily remove it. It was minute, one of those transparent, barely visible kinds. The culprit probably planted itself by working its way through my gloves when I pruned roses or as I transferred the branches to my truck.

Firmly planted in the ball of my thumb, I could feel its presence whenever I applied pressure. The little monster plagued me for several weeks. Removal remained impossible as the recovery mechanism of my body had healed over it. The thorn wasn't visible. Felt, but unseen.

Unresolved grievances hide like thorns or slivers within our beings. You can't see them by looking at a person. People often spend a great amount of time and effort to cover them up, dig a deep hole and bury them, all while striving to keep them invisible and pretending they don't exist. However, when an encounter involving a "touchy" subject takes place, a volatile, negative reaction may spew forth. "Where did that come from?" an observer may wonder.

Two categories of grievances exist: perceived wrongs and valid ones.

Perceived wrongs fulfill that description exactly — personal injury or hurt based on *my* perception, how *I* saw a situation or experience, void of the truth and reality. For example, the abrupt, rude clerk or waitress at the store or restaurant. The unknown factor: They may have just received news of a terminal illness in their family. Perhaps the driver of the vehicle who just cut off traffic, going at breakneck speed, was on their way to the emergency room. Maybe an acquaintance who ignored you in the grocery store wasn't snubbing you but just had a knock-down, drag-out argument with her husband or child. None of these have a personal basis.

Valid grievances differ from perceived ones. Their base comes from personal injury, damage, or hurt—physical or otherwise—at the hand of another.

However, it does not matter a whit which of those we carry within our being, perceived or valid. If one does not deal with a grievance, it festers and grows.

I daresay carrying a personal grievance is an all-too-familiar situation, sometimes lasting throughout a lifetime. They begin in early infancy, a baby expressing protest over being placed in bed against their will. "It's not fair!" is an often-heard outcry in a family, whether because of a sibling being given perceived favored treatment or when being told "no."

Fast-forward to adulthood, and things really don't change. Labor unions and employers have a detailed, intricate system to deal with grievance issues. In business relationships, marriages, and friendships, it seems someone is always experiencing hurt.

When comparing one's life with another, an unspoken assessment may result: "They had everything given to them. Life's so unfair!"

Have you heard the comment, "I may forgive, but I don't forget"? That statement expresses my point exactly—grievances held against another, be it a spouse or family member, friend, employer, the government, minister, or any fellow citizen. They silently stack up within a person, tainting the quality of one's life.

I am going to address another point in this discussion, though, that of holding a grievance against God. I maintain the crux of what we deem as personal is, in truth, directed toward Him. While not always an easy truth to see, and it means digging deep, the anger people hold against God many times spills over into rage. Issues held against Him, they cry out, "Why do You allow so much hardship, tragedy, loss, poverty, war? Why did You allow my beloved family member or friend to become ill and suffer? Why did You take their life?" Humankind lacks understanding and control. Ergo, it becomes personal. In the natural state of being human, people readily cast blame on Him, never forgiving or forgetting.

How does one deal with grievance and experience healing, living free of the venom it produces within a person? How can one even be made aware? Seek truth, light, and life. Seek God. Healing and freedom can be found only in Him and Him alone.

My thumb has healed. I'm always pleasantly surprised at the difference removal of a finite object makes. The same goes for my inner spiritual being.

On Forgiveness and Healing

You took my broken heart and made it whole.
You took my shattered life. You healed my soul.
You gave me hope.
You gave me strength so I could carry on.

I was so all alone. No place to call my own, my home.
I placed my life into Your hands. A childish trust, not one I'd planned.
You filled a void in me, gave me eyes to see.
You gave me peace within.

You wrapped me in Your arms.
You held me close, free from harm.
You whispered in my ear, so soft that I could barely hear:
"Forgive, My child, and be healed."

My heart sings out to You for all eternity.
The wounds, the hurts are but a memory.
But this I know, I know forevermore:
"Forgive, My child, and be healed."

On Being Prepared

prepare: v. To make ready for a specific future purpose; to set up.

Weed eater in tow, I headed to edge the lawn before mowing. *Thankfully, I'm not going to be doing this forever* passed through my mind. The thought brought me some solace. As a self-employed gardener, I've mowed that same lawn scores of times. The repetitiveness week after week, year after year, can be mentally taxing. And forever *is* a long, long time.

One of my pregnancies took place during the heat of summer. In addition to the usual effects of pregnancy, allergies plagued me. Out of concern for my unborn child, I refused to take any form of medication for the ravaging attacks. The sneezing; perpetual runny nose; scratchy, irritated eyes; and general malaise associated with them made everyday life difficult and miserable during the final months. In addition, the little one decided to delay entrance into the world ten days past her due date.

Mentally, I determined the pregnancy would last forever. The point wasn't open for discussion. Even if such a debate took place, no one could have convinced me otherwise. Logic would not have prevailed. I *knew* I was going to be pregnant for a long, long time. Period.

Thankfully, God's ordination for birth superseded my crazed imaginations. I did not have to prepare for a "forever" pregnancy, but for the birth of my daughter.

Forever *is* a long, long time. How does one prepare for *forever*? Most of life's preparations center around here and now. Or even the future. But not forever.

We live in a society and a culture where the importance of being prepared for potential situations is stressed. In fact, promoting preparedness creates fortunes for the business world.

The base premise of the sales pitch used by insurance salesmen emphasizes the need to be prepared for the possibility of any variety of scenarios. Americans spend an exorbitant amount of money on insurance protection of all types. We pay for insurance policies "in case of" earthquakes, flooding, fire, automobile accidents, death, and more. Death *is* the only inevitable one.

Humankind makes every effort to be ready for every possible hypothetical situation from the beginning of life to its end.

Many parents begin preparing for their child's college education and its expense at the time of birth by setting up a college fund. Some begin in infancy, making certain they place their child in the "right" school from nursery school through high school so they will be accepted into the "right" college. I would call this preparation at its finest.

Some people keep a stockpile of food and cash on hand out of fear the electrical grid could become disabled. Alarm systems in our homes and/or the possession of personal firearms have become common methods of dealing with the possibility of intruders. Investors diversify their stock portfolios in order to ensure the ups and downs of the stock market have the least possible adverse effect. Families put plans of action in place so if disaster strikes the members know where to meet and what to do.

Flu shots, annual health exams, gym memberships all exist in the hope of averting any adverse physical conditions or disease. We prepare for the end of life with wills, funeral plans, and directives for when we may not be able to express our will concerning physical care.

I believe humans have been created as eternal beings. While our physical life, the short-term one, may last several decades, perhaps nine or even ten, the next life, the long-term one, extends into infinity.

We are "forever" beings. Physical death of the body does not bring about the end. Rather, each of us will take a step into the next dimension with a single, final breath and heartbeat. That dimension consists of all that is real, with more substance than anything we see or experience with our physical eyes.

I have no goal or desire to try to convince you of something you disagree with and do not believe. However, it *is* my goal and desire to challenge you to question the truth and merit of what I say.

Take a single step back. Look. Consider. Evaluate. What if? Given the fact of the brevity of our physical life in comparison to the length of the next one . . . what if people prepared for long-term with even a small amount of the time, energy, and thought given in preparation for short-term? Let me see. Ninety years vs. infinity. From a place of pure logic and common sense, which warrants the greater attention?

How does a person prepare for forever? Humans cannot prepare themselves for eternity. Preparation must take place at the hand of God as we mortals seek Him in sincerity and truth.

May you be prepared for the time you enter into His presence.

Forever *is* a long, long time.

> *The LORD is near to all who call on him,*
> *to all who call on him in truth.*
> Psalm 145:18

I Wonder

wonder: v. To think or speculate curiously; to ponder; to feel doubt and curiosity; to query in the mind; be curious to know.

"Inquiring minds want to know." This phrase, used in the 1970s ad for an American tabloid called *The National Enquirer*, is often applied to curious people.

None of us have all the answers to life or *in* life. In fact, we often live our lives with more questions than answers. Wondering fits in that place between knowing something beyond a shadow of a doubt and not having a clue. Should wondering be placed in the same category as having an inquiring mind? Perhaps.

I spend much of my worktime as a gardener alone in thought, which includes a great deal of wondering. Wondering is not the equivalent of worrying. Nor do these thoughts fall in the category of "need to know," with a pressing urgency. When I engage in that state, I am not on a search for truth or driven to find an answer. Rather, the thoughts tend to enter unannounced and leave quietly, without my drawing any conclusion. They cover a wide variety of subject matter, from the silly and frivolous to the heavy and serious.

I wonder: Why can't I train myself to keep better track of my hand tools when I'm working? I lose pruners, hand scythes, and other tools because I simply drop them on the ground, without thinking, when I've finished using them. On a good day, I'll notice them and set them in a visible place. On other days, I strongly suspect I've raked them up and discarded them along with the yard debris.

When I come to the end of a swath of lawn while mowing, why do I often go in a circle rather than making a simple pivot to head back the opposite direction? Why don't I dress more appropriately according to the weather? Why don't I remember to take food and water with me and use sunscreen *before* I get sunburned? Why do I love planting a garden but tending it not so much?

When I hear music coming from a vehicle passing by that is so loud I can feel its thumping, rhythmic vibrations inside my house, I always wonder: How can the occupants of the car tolerate that kind of volume? What are they trying to drown out in their own minds? How has their hearing been affected?

I often find my curiosity piqued about the backstory of individuals who either collect bottles and cans or stand on street corners with signs asking for money. Two young men, a set of twins, scour the neighborhood, filling shopping carts and large garbage bags with their bounty of recyclable containers to cash in. I ask myself how it came to be that twins would end up in the same situation, living hand-to-mouth? What circumstances brought them to that place? We are all sons and daughters with a mother and a father, a childhood, and perhaps siblings. These folk do not differ. They went to school somewhere, had goals and aspirations at some time in their lives, and probably still do. Everyone has a story, and I wonder about those I see.

As one in her eighties, I find myself viewing my future in a way I never have before. I view time differently than when I was thirty or forty, or even sixty. What awaits me in this physical life? And how much longer will I have that life?

I often think about life after death, the next step after the physical body experiences a final heartbeat and a last breath. What takes place then? Even though I'm familiar with biblical passages and have read several accounts of near-death experiences, I have no preconceived ideas, thoughts, or fairy-tale images of the hereafter. I am left wondering.

What is hell like? Again, I don't know. More unknowns. More questions. For me, any place without God constitutes hell. But that's just my perspective.

I have pondered what the drama of Creation looked like. I hope God allows me to see a rerun of it someday. I would like to watch as He spoke and light came upon what was without form and covered in darkness. I would like to see it all in slow motion, to witness as He placed the sun, the moon, the stars, gathered the water to form the seas, and created our continents from the remaining dry land, Will He let me?

Our world has become so consumed with saving the planet and serving and preserving self that the most important treasure is being cast away with total disregard, the hearts and souls of men. Scripture describes this state as worshiping the creation instead of the Creator.[22] In addition, what does the future hold for a world of people who not only have no regard for the One who gave them life but scorn Him and treat Him with contempt and disdain?

---

[22] Romans 1:25

Recently, I have wondered if God feels like flicking all of mankind off the face of the earth with His finger. He did it once before, you know, when He opened the fountains of the deep and caused it to rain for forty days and forty nights. He brought about the flood and its destruction after He looked upon mankind "and saw that the wickedness of humans was great in the earth . . . and the LORD was sorry that he had made humans on the earth, and it grieved him to his heart."[23] How does He feel as He looks upon humankind now?

What would you do if you were in His place? God is love. He is also long-suffering and patient. That can come to an end, though. Not only did he destroy the earth with a flood, He also rained down burning sulfur[24] to wipe out Sodom and Gomorrah because their sin grieved Him so badly.

These are things to take seriously . . . and not just wonder about.

May God have mercy on us.

---

[23] Genesis 6:5–6
[24] Genesis 18:20; 19:24

On What If?

The old-timers would have called it a "gully washer," the kind of rain where the windows of heaven open and water pours down in sheets. A person caught out in it unprepared becomes "bone-drenched" in a matter of minutes.

I needed to remove the leaves from the law office sidewalks, and I came prepared, wearing my rain gear. The job needed to be done on Saturday, rather than the usual Sunday. I had a very important Sunday commitment, a trip to the Portland airport to pick up my grandgirl. Postponing the work was not an option, so I gritted my teeth and proceeded to deal with the last of the season's fallen leaves.

Glancing up, I saw my client motioning me from the building's lovely veranda with the silent message, *"Come, get out of the rain."*

I accepted his invitation, and so we sat on the porch benches and visited, protected from the torrential downpour

We have had an amiable employer/employee relationship for several years, and I usually tend his office grounds on weekends to avoid noise intrusion. We've visited often, sharing the activities and events in the lives of our families and our personal lives. That kind of exchange took place once again as we discussed Thanksgiving plans, the food, and those with whom we would share the day. The reality of change became a topic front and center as we compared the growth and development of children and grandchildren.

At some point in the conversation, he stated emphatically, "I believe in one less god than most. I also believe that at the end of this life we all just become compost." I remained silent, neither expressing my point of view nor attempting to dissuade him.

That comment, however, provided fodder for thought in the ensuing days. Why does humankind assume if they preface a statement with "I believe," it somehow makes it absolute, that *truth* is stamped upon one's personal credo with those two words?

A difference of chasmic proportions exists between what "I believe" and truth. I know, because I was challenged in my twenties to question, search, and seek out the reality and validity of truth. Nothing else matters. Only truth will stand and endure, not only under the test of time and the circumstances of everyday life, but all eternity. So much of what I once believed fell away as truth took its place. I have never ceased in that quest.

A friend shared a pearl of wisdom, one I've never forgotten: "You can believe whatever you want. You can believe with all your heart that the moon is made of blue cheese, but that doesn't make it so."

And so, that Saturday afternoon conversation left me with a question, one applicable to each of us: What if? What if a person's beliefs consist of only that—a personal belief, nothing more, nothing less? What if my beliefs have no correlation to the truth? What if they fall in the same category as that of believing the moon is made of blue cheese? This important question deserves consideration.

Personally, I know the way I want to live. I want my life

to be built on truth rather than on the dogma of man, the ever-fluid positions of science or a personal "belief." The difference is stark—building on sand compared to building on a solid rock.

My challenge to you: Question, search, and seek all that is true. Truth can only be found by going to the One who *is* truth, Almighty God.

What if?

> *When you search for me, you will find me;*
> *if you seek me with all your heart.*
> Jeremiah 29:13

On the Endgame

endgame: n. The final stage of an extended process or course of events.

one's A game: n. One's highest level of play or performance.

Pruning the massive climbing rose in my client's yard held my total concentration. The sound of a voice startled me and caught me off-guard. "Ladonna . . ." Following the sound, I turned toward the source. The upper portion of his head, with thinning hair and bright eyes, revealed his presence as he peeked over the top of the fence. Gary is a former landscaper and a peer. When I work in his neighbor's garden, the topics of our over-the-fence conversations often consist of either gardening or subjects relating to our age, since we both qualify as "seniors."

Even though the calendar says "spring," the area where I live on Oregon's Willamette Valley floor has experienced a never-ending winter this year. Spring days with sunny warmth have been few and far between. We lamented that fact, as gardeners do. He told me about his recent knee replacement surgery and the recuperative process and progress.

Those of us in our senior years share the common experience of an acceleration of time. We readily concurred: Time *is* passing at the speed of light. We talked about the reality of being a "senior" and the brief amount of time left in our lives. "We're all on the same conveyor belt," he said, "and when it stops, it stops." He expressed his belief that when death comes, nothing follows.

When the citizens of the world crack their eyes open as they awaken in the morning, most do not have the knowledge that "today is the last day I am going to live life on this earth." Yet daily, as surely as the sun rises and sets, death, the end of physical life, becomes the personal experience of tens of thousands of people around the world, regardless of age or station in life.

In the sports world, the endgame, the last few seconds of play, carries the hope and possibility of a win for the team facing loss. In football, a last-ditch effort to score might be attempted with a Hail Mary pass. In basketball, a three-point shot may be hurled from center court with the hope of coming out the victor. In games such as bridge or chess, the endgame occurs in the final stage when few pieces or cards remain, and they need to be played carefully in order to win. How, then, can that term have a spiritual application?

My mother, in the throes of Alzheimer's with rare moments of lucidity and voice, told me of an experience she had. Some would call it a vision. "I was walking down a road," she said, "and I came up to a door. The door opened, and there He stood, just as big as life."

"Who?" I asked.

"Well, God," she answered. "Who do you think?"

"Were you afraid?"

"Well, no. Should I have been?" And she spoke no more.

This *is* the endgame for each person alive . . . one last step, one last breath before that door opens and we enter into eternity.

Perhaps one has lived life with very little thought given to or about God. Life revolves around so many activities in such a busy social schedule, with people to see, places to visit, bucket list items to be fulfilled, and goals to be reached, that no room or time remains for Him.

Oftentimes people speak of living each day as though it were their last by focusing on the treatment of friends and family. I would suggest the attention be turned the opposite direction—toward God since He *is* the final destination.

The time will arrive when no more chess pieces or cards remain, no more plays can be made. Life will be over. Be prepared for the inevitable, the unavoidable. Make certain your endgame is your A game, one where God is the focus.

Consider your life—past, present, and future—in the light, truth, and reality of God and eternity.

> *"'This very night your life is being demanded of you.*
> *And the things you have prepared, whose will they be?'*
> *So it is with those who store up treasures for themselves*
> *but are not rich toward God."*
> Luke 12:20–21

Do You Know My Father?

Do you know my Father?
Do you know my friend?
He loves me.
My life is in His hands.

He's a loving Father.
He is kind and true.
He will never fail you.
He's waiting just for you.

Will you meet my Father?
Will you meet my friend?
He loves you too.
Is your life in His hands?

About the Author

Ladonna Shanks was born and raised in Oregon's lush Willamette Valley. She graduated with high honors from Lebanon High School many decades ago then married and raised her family—a son and three daughters. She is now an official "elder" after turning eighty as 2025 began. During her several decades of life, she has pursued many interests, calling herself "a Jill-of-all-trades, mistress of none." She has been an entrepreneur—a struggling one, a small business owner, operating a gardening business for twenty years until retirement in 2022, and, most recently, a writer. Her first book, *Tidbits and Pearls: A Book of Essays on Living Everyday Life with God*, was published in 2019. Ladonna's family, including five grandgirls, and her commitment to God serve as her priorities. Not to be forgotten is her love of laughter. You may contact the author at shankstidbits@gmail.com.

www.ingramcontent.com/pod-product-compliance
Lightning Source LLC
Chambersburg PA
CBHW030449100526
44580CB00002B/57